WITHDRAWN FROM LIBRARY

Equal parts elegy, tragedy and history, Rafferty traces the distance between regret and remembering, and by doing so, writes his own monument; one that reminds us of what we've lost, and what we don't dare lose again.

B. J. HOLLARS, author of *This Is Only a Test*

Thoughtful and insightful, Rafferty deftly and playfully weaves cultural and personal narrative into a book that is not just enlightening, but a pure pleasure to read. Colin Rafferty is an excellent guide down the rabbit hole and into this wonderland of physical objects our culture has built to help us remember both disaster and heroism.

SHERYL ST. GERMAIN, author of *Navigating Disaster: Sixteen Essays of Love and a Song of Despair*

Colin Rafferty has written about the spaces between 'before' and 'after,' time and place, memory and imagination, fact and story. He acts as a guide across our land and beyond to show us how we stand before the monument or the memorial to remember what has been forgotten, [illegible] happened, and to

D1004364

separate history from mythology. These essays reveal how the words "On this site" can never bring back all that happened, but they can resurrect the phantoms that haunt our history, both private and public. *Hallow This Ground* is a stunning and moving tour through history and memory, loss and love, and ultimately, through the desire to wonder after what's true so we might better know ourselves.

JILL TALBOT, author of *The Way We Weren't: A Memoir*

These essays, wondrous in their scope, travel far and wide to deftly inquire something this reader never really considered—what is a monument? The effect of following Colin Rafferty through shipwreck sites, presidential birthplaces, death camps, and into his growing understanding of body, memory, and self, is nothing short of—dare I say it?—monumental.

ELENA PASSARELLO, author of *Let Me Clear My Throat*

HALLOW THIS GROUND

break away books

Michael Martone

HALLOW *This* GROUND

Colin Rafferty

INDIANA UNIVERSITY PRESS

Bloomington & Indianapolis

This book is a publication of

Indiana University Press
Office of Scholarly Publishing
Herman B Wells Library 350
1320 East 10th Street
Bloomington, Indiana 47405 USA

iupress.indiana.edu

© 2015 by Colin Rafferty
All rights reserved

No part of this book may be reproduced or utilized in any form or by any means, electronic or mechanical, including photocopying and recording, or by any information storage and retrieval system, without permission in writing from the publisher. The Association of American University Presses' Resolution on Permissions constitutes the only exception to this prohibition.

The paper used in this publication meets the minimum requirements of the American National Standard for Information Sciences—Permanence of Paper for Printed Library Materials, ANSI Z39.48–1992.

Manufactured in the United States of America

Cataloging information is available from the Library of Congress.

ISBN 978-0-253-01907-3 (paperback)
ISBN 978-0-253-01913-4 (ebook)

1 2 3 4 5 20 19 18 17 16 15

For Elizabeth

Their monument sticks like a fishbone
in the city's throat.

ROBERT LOWELL, "For the Union Dead"

CONTENTS

Acknowledgments *xiii*

Afterward: An Introduction *1*

A for Absence *10*
Surfacing *13*

A for Ancestry *28*
The Path *31*

A for Answers *44*
Notes Toward Building the Memorial in Somerset County, Pennsylvania *46*

A for Anatomy *56*
Victims: The Yellow Flowers *59*
Bystanders: The End of the World *74*
Perpetrators: Undrawn Lines *93*

A for Ache *108*
The Definite Article *111*

A for Accident *125*
This Day in History *128*
Doors *141*

A for Accumulation *157*
What I Was Doing There *160*
Phantoms (A Correspondence) *175*
Reflecting Mirror: Orlando, the Day After *180*
Hallow This Ground *183*

Aftermath: A Conclusion *197*

Notes *203*

ACKNOWLEDGMENTS

Thank you to the journals in which these essays first appeared: "Surfacing," in *Fourth Genre: Explorations in Nonfiction*; "Notes Toward Building the Memorial in Somerset County, Pennsylvania," in *Witness* (as "Notes Toward Building the Memorial"); "The Yellow Flowers," in *Fourth River*; "The End of the World," in *New Orleans Review*; "This Day in History," in *Sou'wester*; "Doors," in *Crab Orchard Review*; "Phantoms (a Correspondence)," in *Bellingham Review*, and reprinted in *Utne Reader*; and "Reflecting Mirror: Orlando, the Day After," in the anthology *Tuscaloosa Runs This*. In addition, "Surfacing" and "Notes Toward Building the Memorial" were named Notable Essays in *The Best American Essays 2011* and *2013*, respectively.

Thanks, too, go to the editors of these literary journals, who never backed down from strange typographies and layouts, and whose pens improved what was underneath the submissions: Marcia Aldrich, Amber Withycombe, Marc Nieson, Sheila Squillante, John Biguenet, Valerie Vogrin, Jon Tribble, Carolyn Alessio, Brenda Miller, and Keith Goetzman. Double thanks go to Brian Oliu for letting me write "Reflecting Mirror" at his kitchen table.

My parents, Tom and Kathie Rafferty, took me to interesting places, let me check out any book I wanted from the library, and loved tourist kitsch (WORLD'S LARGEST PRAIRIE DOG 8 MILES AHEAD). Thanks, too, to my sister, Mollie, who was always along for the ride.

I was lucky to have great teachers along the way: Sharon Nehls, Melissa Reynolds, Christopher Cokinos, Stephen Pett, Sheryl St. Germain, Debra Marquart, Wendy Rawlings, Joyelle McSweeney, Diane Roberts, Joel Brouwer, and Fred Whiting. Thanks especially go to Michael Martone, who deserves a monument of his own made from Bedford limestone.

Thanks to the friends who read drafts of these, especially Brian Oliu, Jennifer Pemberton, Patrick Scott Vickers, Alissa Nutting, and Braden Welborn.

I am indebted to everyone at Break Away Books and Indiana University Press, especially Sarah Jacobi, Darja Malcolm-Clarke, and Jill R. Hughes, for taking an idea I had and giving it a literal form and shape.

Many thanks go to George Wolfe, whose Wolfe Travel Grant at the University of Alabama allowed me to travel to Poland and Germany to do research for this book.

When I started writing these essays, I thought I had to write about historical traumas because I had none of my own; that had changed by the time I completed the book. In a way, this book is for Glenda Braun, Bobbie Scrivner, Claudia Emerson, David Steinberg, Marjorie Braun, and Austin Wade.

Finally, thank you to Elizabeth Wade, travel companion on the road, in the air, and in life, who, in front of the plaque in Prague marking where Jan Palach set himself on fire to protest the Communist regime, looked at me and said, "You know, it's two days before Christmas. Could we do something Christmasy next?" Thank you for the next.

HALLOW THIS GROUND

Afterward

AN INTRODUCTION

These things usually start with a date, so:

On February 26, 2000, my mother's fiftieth birthday, I found myself staring up at pieces of plywood in an exurb of Denver, Colorado. The plywood covered some windows that had been broken on purpose almost a year earlier and would stay in place until completion of renovations, a few months away.

From my remove, I shoved my hands a little deeper into my coat's pockets, trying to block out the wind that swept down from the foothills of the Rockies. I was out of my way; my parents live in Boulder, about a half hour from Denver physically and a million miles away in temperament. Driving up here, I'd left the billboard-free, chain-disdaining environs of Boulder County for the strip mall wonderland of Jefferson County.

A temporary trailer, the kind used on construction sites—*this is a construction site,* I reminded myself—stood to the right of the boarded-up windows. It served, I'd read, as the school's temporary library. I thought about all of those books inside, what they'd seen, each one of them marked permanently with the scars of where they'd come from, a smudged stamp on the inside cover reading *Columbine High School Library.*

The library was in the process of being destroyed. The process had started on April 20, 1999, when two students, Eric Harris and Dylan Klebold, improvising an attack after their homemade bombs had failed to explode, opened fire on their classmates. After killing two students outside the school, they moved inside to the library, where they killed ten students before killing themselves.

I have no connection to Columbine—I'm not an alumnus, I didn't grow up in the area, I don't know anyone who went there. And yet I'm here, taking hours out of a short trip home to wish my mother a happy birthday, here to see the place, here to see what they're going to do with it, here to see what happens afterward.

* * *

I wish I could tell you that this fascination with the scene of the crime, with the sites of history and what remains there, has been a temporary thing, a brief fixation in my head on how concrete and steel and granite help us remember, but I've always been this way. I grew up in a family where I didn't go to Disneyland until I was twenty-three but had made it to Vicksburg and Little Big Horn battlefields by age fifteen. Had I been on the Universal Studios Tour? No. But I had been to the Number Nine Saloon in Deadwood, South Dakota, and seen the chair Wild Bill

Hickok was sitting in when he'd been shot. On the Vicksburg trip I obsessed not over the battle itself or the raised gunboat *Cairo,* but the monuments on the battlefield each state had built to its soldiers—Illinois's massive sanctuary with its granite dome, my home state of Kansas' wiry abstract nonsense with three circles unbroken and broken. At the age of ten I told an autograph dealer that the plaque he had labeling a signature misidentified Lincoln as the seventeenth president; he was, of course, the sixteenth. This reveals two things about me, as far as I can tell: first, that I was the kind of ten-year-old who knew that Lincoln was the sixteenth president, and, second, that I was the kind of ten-year-old kid who would revel in getting to show up an adult with that knowledge of history.

So I grew up a happy kid, I think. Nothing of the kinds of drama that make for a good memoir happened to me: no abuse, no drugs, no wild sex parties in the basement. My parents stayed married—they still are—and if they had problems, they did an excellent job of keeping them from me and my little sister. Death visited us infrequently and always at a remove from my life—a grandfather or a great-aunt, not a friend or a parent. I had some friends in school, and although I wasn't the most popular, I got along well enough with most people.

From this I grew into an adult who mostly kept to a small circle of friends. I was personable enough with strangers, but had, as therapists like to say, difficulty "opening up" to people close to me. If I were to diagnose myself—and I suppose this book is in part my attempt to do so obliquely—I'd guess that I had a combination of Midwestern reticence combined with a belief that my problems weren't anything to go on about, that I really didn't have anything worth complaining about.

I did not believe in my own traumas, so I took on those of others. I found that I had a habit of slowing down when driving past historical markers on the road, trying to read them. Often they were dull—formations of associations and signings of town charters—but sometimes they would reveal a surprise: an old-time barnstorming game between the Red Sox and the hometown team in the middle of Kansas, the creation of a new kind of blue cheese on the campus of Iowa State University.

Whenever trauma happened, I often followed a few days later. A day after the World Trade Organization riots, I walked around the streets of Seattle among graffitied Gaps and smashed-up McDonald's. When someone burst into a shipping office and opened fire, killing two, I looked not for the murderer, still at large, but for the building, on a road I drove often. And when I returned to Colorado after the Columbine shooting, I drove out to Littleton and, tracing with my eyes the steps the killers took, stood staring at the library in the process of being ripped out and replaced with an atrium, a memorial.

This informal tour of the dead, of things done and commemorated, grew, sites linking together. I read book after book, trying to catch up with history. I relocated from state to state, moving around, immersing myself into each place's history because I didn't know how else to feel like I lived there. In other countries I sought out and studied their monuments and memorials. I developed a taxonomy: we called it a "monument" when we remembered a triumph, a "memorial" when we remembered a tragedy (DC has a Washington Monument and a Lincoln Memorial, because even though each man died in bed, Washington had a throat infection, and Lincoln had a bullet in his brain).

And what has come of it, of this wandering obsession, of this leaving my family and loved ones to sift through the way we negotiate collective histories? Just these words, these fragments shored against the ruins of history, against bones and blood covered up with glass and concrete and steel.

* * *

I think of what follows as a series of personal essays and not exactly a memoir. I am less *I* and more *eye* in them, an observer trying to consider the significance of how we remember, to watch the twentieth century's mad rush to commemorate itself.

But I am a different eye than those with which we normally regard these structures. There is always a prescribed way to move through these events, a reaction the artists and architects expect us to have, an emotion—sorrow, regret, occasionally joy—that they try to make us feel. I wanted to move beyond that, to disrupt that intended experience and get to a different meaning. I wasn't trying to be a proxy for anyone when I went to these places. I was trying to become myself, and to do that I had to leave behind the tour groups and their designated mourners. No matter how much I try simply to observe, my life bleeds through. There are a few threads here, scaffolding that I've left up to connect these dates and times, intersections of my own small-h *history* with capital-H *History*. If you tilt it at the right angle, it might look like memoir to you. Sometimes it does to me.

So let's mark the date and place: Littleton, Colorado, on the twenty-sixth of February 2000. I didn't want to go back to my apartment, a thousand miles away. There was a girl there, and I was living with her, at least for a little longer. We were in transition, decay, entropy. I had to go on, I had to go home. The monuments were facts; they were done, over, completed. They were stone and steel points marked on a graph, *x*-axis of time and *y*-axis of place. We, on the other hand, had to keep going on with our lives.

She would leave, and she would leave scars. And there are more women in this book, but maybe they should be read as essays as well, my attempt to craft a narrative between myself and someone else. They were almost always there in the process of writing, and they haunt the battlefields.

* * *

Consider the stone knives in a Neanderthal's grave or the dried flowers, still with a bit of color in them, laid upon the breast of an Egyptian mummy, and you'll understand that we've always been a species given over to following death with remembrance, that the worst fate for us is to be forgotten after dying. The monuments built to the memory of the dead stagger our senses with their attempts to negate death's effect, from the pyramids at Giza, to the Taj Mahal, to the fields of tombstones in Western Europe and the American South.

And we do this with art—art made not for someone's house, but for a public space. Monuments and memorials are meant to be experienced both aesthetically and historically, to affect us in more ways than a museum's collection or historian's work can. We place tremendous pressure on them to do these tasks, an almost impossible charge to hold back the inevitable, to accomplish the impossible.

In memorializing the dead, the living seek to erase death, to keep the dead on the earth through sheer force of memory, to keep them alive forever, their souls residing in building materials. And in doing so the living also try to heal themselves of the knowledge of the means of dying, to have it make an ordered sense, a stay against confusion. Where a field became a slaughterhouse now stand row after row of crosses; where a bomb exploded, a peaceful garden.

And so it happens that you might stop while driving, in the city or in the country, in front of a granite tablet or bronze marker and read three words to explain the set-aside grass in front of you: *On this site . . .*

* * *

The prescription is to erase. Torn down: the San Ysidro McDonald's where twenty-one people died, a monument built on the spot. The house where Megan Kanka was raped and murdered, now a children's park. The Broad Arrow Café in Tasmania—twenty dead—replaced by a sculpture. The library at Columbine, converted into an atrium for the cafeteria beneath it. An open field where Jeffrey Dahmer's apartment building stood. A garden at the site of the Dunblane school gymnasium. The Mount Carmel compound outside of Waco. The Murrah Federal Building in Oklahoma City. The World Trade Center. When they tore down Sandy Hook Elementary, they hid the demolition with a fence, as though we could not bear more destruction at the site of destruction.

When death comes on the grandest of scales, the survivors remove the debris, smooth over the dirt, take away the proof that whatever happened did so because to leave it there would create a kind of remembering too much to bear, a remembering too raw and unmitigated. The memorial is the conduit of memory, a resistor of history, ohms of commemoration shielding us from the shock of the world, a way of saving the living from the dead. From death.

* * *

Let me start by asking a question.

After the little evidence flags have been plucked from the spots where they stood guard over shells and bits of broken glass; after the report, voluminous and heavy, issues forth from the investigative agencies; after the endless asking, the who and how and why of it all, especially the *why,* always the *why,* grows quiet; after the teary-eyed tributes in the local newspaper vanish, given back over to holiday sales and crossword puzzles; after the white or blue or green or any other color ribbons have been unpinned and placed in drawers; after the dedications stop coming into the radio station and the updates stop appearing in the national news; after the last flame of the candlelight vigils winks out, leaving behind a curl of smoke in the darkness; after the camera crews return to the stations with their footage, no longer fed live to the networks; after the last survivor emerges from the crawlspace; after the drivers of the wounded speed to the hospital, sirens afire; after the last gunshot rings in the building like a child's cry; after the police enter, guns drawn and aimed at the unknown; after the windows have shaken with each blast; after the first squad car arrives, burning black onto the street where it stops; after the people in hiding throw a garbage can through a window or climb through the air ducts to make an escape route; after one person is allowed to leave unscathed while another dies; after the quiet regard and then the storm; after the hammer falls on the firing pin for the very first time; after the first confused moments; after the grief; after the fear; after the confusion; after the unknowing, what is to be done?

Just this:

A for Absence

Memory fails me, us. Our emotions fade until, like reconciling lovers, we no longer remember what upset us in the first place. But a physical object—the monument—reminds us every time we encounter it, holds up the event we have forgotten so that we might recall what happened, so that we do not forget. And the monuments we call memorials are for things that we'd rather forget: our failings, our accidents, our regressing into our primitive selves. Happy things we have little problem remembering, but with sorrows, mistakes, we must worry the wounds.

The body provides us with our own histories, of the moments when we breach our boundaries, inflict damage upon ourselves or have it inflicted upon us by others. The scars that cover us tell us our story. American Unitarian minister and social reformer

Minot Judson Savage wrote that "a man's truest monument must be a man," and although he meant morally, that a man must craft his own history through his own actions, I cannot help but think of the crisscrossing scars that mark our bodies.

They are there, even if we cannot see them in certain light or from certain angles. Each one of us, covered in the history of our lives, both how we were injured and how we repaired ourselves. The scars are our own personal monuments. They take, generally, two shapes—either a circle (a sewing needle, a vaccination, a bullet wound) or a line (paper cuts, scratches, a knife's blade across a vein). In the vanishing language of Morse code, disappearing because it is merely sound and touch, lost in the instance after it occurs because it lacks a lasting physical presence; in that code a circle followed by a line—dot-dash—is *A*. Alpha, the beginning. We begin our lives with the wound of the umbilical's severance, leaving behind a physical reminder of our origin, the evidence of things not seen.

After college, aimlessly existing in a city, I worked at a record store, a job I hated for the snobbish cool of my hipster coworkers. One day, while I was closing the cash register drawer, the thin skin of my wrist caught on the metal corner. The drawer cut a narrow line, no more than an inch long, diagonally. It bled for a bit, then scabbed over.

I should have forgotten that time of my life by now, forgotten the Bauhaus-loving coworkers and junkie shoplifters and the pay that barely kept me from homelessness. It has been more than a decade since that regrettable job, more than a decade since I worked a job for just two months, and yet as I write this I can look down at my right wrist and see the scar that cash register left. And decades from now, I will look down at my right wrist and still see it.

The ordinary made extraordinary by what happened. Abstract time, fixed in a physical place. The ordinary made memory by the monument. The invisible, given shape and memory by the monument.

Surfacing

On the 25th of March, we took a miserable farewell of our distressed brethren, the heart of every one being so overloaded with his own misery as to have little room to pity another.

R. Thomas, "Preservation of Nine Men,"
Interesting and Authentic Narratives of the Most Remarkable Shipwrecks, 1835

On the eighth of November 1975, a storm forms in Oklahoma and begins moving northeast, picking up speed and intensity. The next day, it passes over Kansas City, over the older suburb of Mission, on the Kansas side of the state line, over a brown house on Nall Avenue where my parents, Tom and Kathie Rafferty, live. Maybe my mother, twenty-five years old and six months pregnant with her first child—me—looks up at the darkening sky and worries. Maybe she feels me moving inside her, pushing her abdomen outward, growing and moving each day. Maybe she stays inside the entire day, unaware of the system passing overhead, not knowing or even caring where it comes from or where it will go.

Ships are certainly far from her mind on this day in Kansas City. She and my father rarely cross the Missouri River, the only major body of water for hundreds of miles. The storm will pass over her, my father, and me, and move on toward Iowa and Wisconsin, growing and moving. Two days after it forms, the storm will arrive at the Great Lakes, bringing with it heavy rains and gale-force winds, all the power it has carried since its birth in Oklahoma. Not long after the storm passes over us, it will strike down twenty-nine men, drowning them in their ship in the middle of the largest lake in the Western Hemisphere, leaving their bodies floating inside the ship, still wrapped in their lifejackets. Then it will continue over Canada, its power fading, until it dissipates, vanishes into the thin air from which it formed.

* * *

Whitefish Point is, quite literally, the end of the road. At the town of Paradise, Michigan, State Highway 123 turns west toward Tahquamenon Falls State Park, and a Chippewa County road, marked as a thin gray line on the state map, continues north until it ends in the parking lot of Whitefish Point's biggest tourist attraction, the Great Lakes Shipwreck Museum. The coast of Lake Superior is just a few yards away.

I have traveled to the Upper Peninsula of Michigan to see a monument that I cannot see: the memorial to the twenty-nine men who died on the *Edmund Fitzgerald* when it sank in a storm on Lake Superior on November 10, 1975. Twenty years later, divers seventeen miles off of Whitefish Point brought up the ship's bell, polished off two decades of rust so that it gleamed again, and hung it as the centerpiece of the museum's collection of artifacts.

But they realized that in removing that bell, they would leave an absence in the ship's wreckage, and they refused to disturb the grave. So they cast another bell, the same shape and size as the *Fitzgerald*'s original, and engraved on it the names of the men who died. Then, after the first bell had been brought up, they lowered down the new bell, and divers with acetylene torches welded it in place.

It's there still, accessible only to divers who are willing to expose themselves to Lake Superior's killing chill. I stand on the shore of Lake Superior in the cold wind of July and look out on choppy water, trying to guess where, seventeen miles north, a memorial sits fixed for the ages 535 feet underwater, a memorial that truly was, as the inscription says but never means, *for the dead.* I think about the thirty thousand people dead in shipwrecks on the Great Lakes, about the twenty-nine men who died when the *Edmund Fitzgerald* sank, and of one man in particular: the ship's steward, an Ohio native named Robert Rafferty.

* * *

On the ninth of November 1975, the *Fitzgerald,* a 729-foot-long cargo vessel, took on just over twenty-six thousand tons of taconite pellets, a low-grade iron ore, at the docks in Superior, Wisconsin. It then set out for Detroit, but to reach it the ship would have to cross Lake Superior. The National Weather Service had issued an alert concerning gale-force winds on the lake that same day, but the *Fitzgerald,* along with several other ships, pushed onward. And why not? The captain, Ernest McSorley, was experienced, as was his crew. His ship, the largest cargo ship ever built when it was launched in 1958, had made the trip plenty of times.

But the barometer kept dropping and the waves kept getting higher. The weather service issued new reports, warning of high winds and thunderstorms on the lake. By the afternoon of the tenth, the winds were up to hurricane force—the *Arthur M. Anderson,* the ship nearest to the *Fitzgerald* when it sank, recorded sustained winds of sixty-seven miles per hour. Waves kept crashing over the bows of both ships, and loaded as they were, it wasn't long before the ships began to pitch and yaw in the waves.

It's difficult for me, and maybe for most people who grew up landlocked, to imagine a boat longer than two football fields being thrown about in a storm. As I look out from Whitefish Point toward the invisible banks of Canada many miles away, I try to imagine eight-foot-high waves rolling through a snowstorm and the building panic as the crew realized how bad the waters were becoming and how much worse they might become.

At 4:30 pm on the tenth, the *Fitzgerald* radioed the *Anderson* and asked them to help them with navigation, as their radar had stopped working. At 6:30 Bernie Cooper, captain of the *Anderson,* saw two waves at least thirty feet high crash over the deck of his ship. His ship was about forty-five minutes away from the *Fitzgerald,* which had already reported a bad list an hour earlier.

At 7:10 the pilot of the *Anderson* radioed the *Fitzgerald* to inform them of another ship on radar, and asked how they were doing.

"We're holding our own," the voice on the other end replied.

A few minutes later the *Fitzgerald* disappeared from the *Anderson's* radar screen. There was no distress call. Two lifeboats, both damaged in a way that suggested they'd been torn from their davits instead of launched by crewmen, were found the next morning, after the *Anderson* and a few other ships whose men were brave enough to risk searching for survivors had sailed through the storm. No bodies were ever recovered.

* * *

Once its respiratory system develops enough, a baby in the womb will begin to breathe, in a manner of speaking. Its lungs will take in the amniotic fluid of the uterus, learning how to inhale and exhale. For nine months a child lives underwater.

When we are born, we scream, proving to the world that we've made the change from water-breather to air-breather. We never make the return trip.

The word "amniotic" descends from the Greek *amnion,* a sacrificial plate to hold a victim's blood. On November 10, 1975, two males with the same last name drew their breath, filling their lungs with fluid. One waited to be born; the other would soon die.

* * *

When I first arrive at Whitefish Point, the power in the museum has failed. According to the staff at the gift shop, this happens fairly regularly—in fact, the same thing happened for a few hours on November 10, 1975, although power was restored before the *Fitzgerald* sank—and the staff tell everyone to wait for a while. People mill around in semidarkness, past sweatshirts and postcards. In a display case, a scale model of the *Fitzgerald* is available for sale.

True to the staff's word, the lights flicker back to life after about fifteen minutes, and I head out of the gift shop, across the lawn, and into the Shipwreck Museum.

My ticket—eight dollars and fifty cents—grants me admission to not only the Shipwreck Museum but also the Whitefish Point Light Station, the oldest active lighthouse on the lake; the Whitefish Point US Coast Guard Lifeboat Station; and a video theater that shows a short film about the *Edmund Fitzgerald* every twenty minutes or so.

The museum itself is simply a single large room filled with artifacts and paintings of ships tossed at sea, recreations of those last desperate moments before they slipped beneath the waves. In the center of the room, sparkling in the light, is the Fresnel lens of a lighthouse, designed to intensify lamplight in the days before the incandescent bulb.

I'm reading a nineteenth-century survivor's tale when the nondescript orchestral music playing softly overhead winds down and a song starts up. The guitarist picks out a simple pattern of notes on his strings, and somewhere in my memory a light flickers on—I've heard this song before, but can't place it anywhere.

"The lake, it is said, never gives up her dead," a man's voice sings from hidden speakers, "when the skies of November turn gloomy."

You've got to be kidding me, I think. *They're playing "The Wreck of the* Edmund Fitzgerald*"? They're playing Gordon Lightfoot? Really?*

Although the ballad's at a fairly low volume, and I'm doing my best to ignore it, I still can't help but notice when, at the end of some verses, Gordon sings the song's title in $\frac{6}{8}$ time—*the WRECK of the EDMUND FitzGERALD!*

The song is now firmly lodged in my brain, where it won't leave until I've driven back over the Mackinac Bridge and off the Upper Peninsula.

More distracted than before, I move in a circle around the room, coming closer and closer to the present day in the museum's chronology. The final exhibit, of course, is about the *Edmund Fitzgerald.* A painting of the ship hangs on the wall, all storm-tossed gloom and drama, and the accompanying text tells the story of the storm that sank the ship nearly thirty years earlier. Rafferty's name—Robert's, not mine—is on a list of the crew. At sixty-two, he was the third-oldest man on the boat, after the captain and the first mate.

Turning away from the exhibit, I see the museum's main attraction: the *Fitzgerald's* bell, brought up by scuba divers ten years earlier. It shines, practically glows, in the light, looking brand-new, not removed from twenty years underwater. The ship's name curves across the metal, and for a moment I want to reach out and touch it, to ring the bell and hear the sound that Rafferty must have heard dozens of times each day. I want to make some sort of connection with Rafferty. Like most memorials, the bell, raised from the ship he died on, is the aid for remembering and connecting with the lost.

On board a ship a bell marks the passage of time, ringing to mark out the hours. This bell marks stopped time, the moment, just after 7:10 pm, on November 10, 1975, when the *Edmund Fitzgerald* slipped under the waves off of Whitefish Point. It remembers the stopped minute, the moment when everything changed. As with all memorials and monuments, it charts, like measurements on a ship's charts, the intersection of time and place.

But this bell, surrounded by artifacts from other shipwrecks, crushed compasses, and faded life rings, is the ersatz memorial for the living to see and navigate their memory by. The true memorial to the dead of the *Edmund Fitzgerald* hasn't been seen in years, could only be seen by a few. The memorial bell, the one 535 feet beneath the waves, serves its function the same way that the plaque one of the Apollo crews left on the moon does; we know it's there, even if we can't reach it. And in a time when everything seems mutable and changing, a time when a ship large enough to hold fifty thousand gallons of fuel can vanish from the face of the earth in less time than it takes to pick up a radio and call for help, the impossible monument, the one we cannot see, reassures us that it remembers.

* * *

I am Colin Rafferty; I am not Robert Rafferty. I am not his son, not his nephew, not his cousin. I am from Kansas City; I am not from Ohio. I grew up landlocked; I am not a sailor. I get seasick, badly, while on a boat. I am a reiteration of Robert Rafferty; I am not a reiteration of Robert Rafferty. I am of his family; I am not of his family. I was born when he died; I breathed in the sea while he choked on it.

* * *

Mark L. Thompson, in his book *Graveyard of the Lakes,* theorizes that Captain McSorley would have ordered his men to don lifejackets and wait in either the forward recreation room or the mess room, depending on where they were when the call came. Since Robert Rafferty was the ship's steward, he most likely would have been in the mess room when the ship went down, and would have either drowned or been crushed by the pressure of the water rushing through the ship.

Rafferty and I might be related, though I can't prove it beyond a hunch and a guess. My several-times-great-grandfather Owen Rafferty came over from County Roscommon, Ireland, during the mass emigrations of the potato famine, and my branch of the Rafferty family passed through both Ohio and Illinois before settling in Carroll County, Iowa, for a number of generations. They came on boats, and once they'd arrived, they moved inland, far away from the seas that tossed them for weeks. They moved to a state where waves meant corn and soybeans, not water. Not something that could drown.

So it's possible that one Rafferty stayed in Ohio while another went to Iowa, or that the gene for mobility that took my father to Kansas City, my uncles to Colorado, and me to Alabama was already in place in the nineteenth century, and someone made his or her way back east from the farms. But I cannot know for sure. The trail of memorials our families leave behind us—properties, tombstones, paperwork—it's all too faint for me to find a path between me and Robert Rafferty, if one even exists.

If a memorial's purpose is to act as a conduit for understanding history, helping those who view it to identify with the victims of whatever's happened, to demonstrate that real lives, individual lives were affected by history, then the *Fitzgerald*'s memorial, a memorial to Robert Rafferty and the rest of the crew, frustrates me. With Robert Rafferty I've found a means to connect personally with the tragedy, to bypass the monument. This could be my family member; I could lay possession to him, call him my own, if I only knew. Without that knowledge, the memorial bell is all I have, a cenotaph, a tombstone without a grave or body.

Robert Rafferty may be my cousin many times removed, or we may share nothing more than a last name. Our relationship is as unknowable to me as the bell engraved with his name and twenty-eight more, ten years sunken and attached to the ship in which his body, lifejacket on, still floats.

* * *

There is some controversy about the *Edmund Fitzgerald*. Three members of the National Transportation Safety Board, in their 1978 report on the accident, blamed the ship's demise on faulty hatch covers that let in water during the course of the storm. The water then settled in the spaces between the taconite pellets, where it couldn't be detected by the sailors, and when the massive wave hit, the ship was already water-laden enough to drop, bow first, to the bottom of the lake.

The board's fourth member, however, wrote a dissenting opinion in which he argued that the ship, carrying a heavy load, had scraped the shoals near Caribou Island and then taken on water. This, he wrote, accounted for the list that McSorley reported. Several authors have written books that attempt to get at the truth of what happened.

But what happened, ultimately, is that twenty-nine men died in a storm on November 10, 1975, and that they were mourned, the bell ringing for them at the Mariners' Church in Detroit the next day. They were the last men to die in a shipwreck in Lake Superior;

for over thirty years now, as long as I've been alive, no one has died the way that Robert Rafferty and his shipmates did.

The US Army Corps of Engineers publishes a fact sheet on the *Fitzgerald.* At the end of it a section for children asks what they would do with their discovery if they were a salvager who raised part or all of the ship. It also states, in the section ostensibly for adults, that the *Fitzgerald* won't be raised and that the men aboard it are considered "buried at sea."

* * *

Here is something I have hidden from you this whole time, something settled in the spaces between these words, something you have not been able to detect: I am not alone at Whitefish Point. My girlfriend, a Michigan native, and I have traveled here together. It was her idea; her grandfather had served in a CCC unit in the Upper Peninsula during the Depression, and she wanted to see the town he'd lived in then.

We have dated for almost three years, the last two at a distance while we earn degrees at different schools. We have talked about marriage; she is ready, more than ready, and in my quiet agreement, we have assumed—both of us—that I am ready, too. She loves me, and she tells me so often. I love her, and I tell her so often.

I will break up with her a few weeks after we return from Whitefish Point.

* * *

What does drowning feel like? I want to hold my head under the water in the bathtub, pushing myself under, trying to understand what that first moment of panic feels like when I need a breath and can't find a place to take one, but I can't bring myself even to try.

The language of drowning is quiet and beautiful; the idea of lungs filling with water a placid image, like a gentle pool fed by a small stream. I'm tempted to think of hundreds of candles in the lungs, each one quietly snuffed out by the rising water. But survivors of near-drownings describe the pain as excruciating. There is a moment of peace, they say, but it doesn't last for long. It's a painful, violent, awful death. My government, the newspaper says, has approved waterboarding, a near-drowning, a simulated drowning, as a means of gathering information from unwilling prisoners.

I can't drown myself in order to understand the sinking of the *Fitzgerald*. What I can do is to look at something taken from the ship itself and try to understand how it can be salvaged after years underwater to tell a story, to remind me of what is lost and what is being lost, what slips under the waves even as we watch, eyes focused on the point where the water meets the sky.

* * *

The Great Lakes Shipwreck Museum also encompasses the old lighthouse station, and after leaving the museum proper, my girlfriend and I tour the house, outfitted with exhibits on the life of the lighthouse keeper.

I'm supposed to say this: it sounds like a lonely existence. The Upper Peninsula receives a massive amount of snowfall each year—mailboxes and outhouses are double-decked here, allowing for usage when the weather forecast calls for seven feet of snow. In the nineteenth century a lighthouse keeper and his family would be virtual exiles for six months out of the year, waiting for the snow to melt enough to reach Paradise, the closest town.

I'll confess this: it's not without its attraction, that solitude, that loneliness.

It's possible now to spend the night at the Coast Guard station at Whitefish Point. What was once a location notable for its proximity to danger, a place from which to launch a rescue or to warn oncoming ships away from the rocks, has also become a place to relax. Next to the Great Lakes Shipwreck Museum is a bird sanctuary; Paradise has a Best Western, and Tahquamenon Falls State Park has its own brewery.

Usually a traumatic event sterilizes the land around it, keeps it from development. But the sinking of the *Edmund Fitzgerald* (and, by extension, the thousands of ships that have sunk in the Great Lakes) have turned Whitefish Point, the end of the road, into a tourist destination, a place people come to forget their troubles by hearing about bigger ones.

* * *

I'm a coward, unable to drown myself and at the same time unable to reach for a life ring. I know and have known that my uncertainty about marriage is a bigger sign than nerves about a ceremony. I spend too much time hating myself for not being able to do it.

When I tell her I cannot, it is fast and sudden. She will have no warning, no time to send out a distress call. It will come upon her suddenly. One Sunday morning, after we are back at our respective universities, with states between us, I will call her. We will talk twice that day, once that morning, once that night. Then I will never hear from her again, three years vanishing under the waves, leaving behind nothing to mark its spot.

* * *

The lake's still choppy, whitecaps breaking as far as the eye can see. On the beach, a couple walks, leaning into the wind to keep their balance. We turn away from the lake and walk over to the video theater, take a seat, and wait for the lights to dim and the video on the *Fitzgerald* to start.

It repeats most of the information from the museum, but nevertheless, it's interesting to see underwater footage of the ship, as well as the bell being brought to the surface. At the end of the video, the ceremony of the bell's installation in the museum plays, and the bell rings thirty times—once for each man who died on the ship, and once for all people who have died in shipwrecks.

Even though I know his name will be read, I'm still surprised to hear the man on the screen intone "Robert Rafferty" and ring the *Fitzgerald's* bell one last time for him. Even on video the sound is loud and seems to ring out for a long time, over the next name, the next peal of the bell, through the darkened room, out its doors into the clear July sky, and over Whitefish Point, traveling at the speed of sound, almost five seconds to a mile, faster than the waves and winds of November 10, toward the spot where the *Edmund Fitzgerald* lies, broken in two by the force of hitting the lake bed, taconite pellets spilled, a spot marked by another bell and, 535 feet above that, the waves breaking over it.

* * *

It will take me until the next spring to develop the roll of film that I shot at Whitefish Point. I find reasons to avoid it, but finally the pictures are developed and I look at them while sitting in my car outside the photo place, the air conditioner running in the already hot air of April.

There is a photo taken from the car as we approach the Mackinac Bridge, and a pair of photos, one of each of us wading in the Tahquamenon River, downstream from the falls. There is a photo of me in front of the Coast Guard station at Whitefish Point, and one of her at the steps leading down to the beach of Lake Superior, her hair blowing sideways in the wind. There are no photos of us together.

A for Ancestry

I am marked by my people.

"For the generations to come every male among you who is eight days old must be circumcised," God tells Abraham as the two of them establish a religion. "My covenant in your flesh is to be an everlasting covenant. Any uncircumcised male, who has not been circumcised in the flesh, will be cut off from his people; he has broken my covenant."

And so the first two scars of my life, the first two events marked in my flesh in the first hours of my existence on this planet, are my entrance to this world and my joining the faith of my fathers—and the faith as expressed by only my fathers. As Catholic males we have had our foreskins removed as a sign of the covenant with God that Abraham made in the Old Testament.

This is strange to talk about in the twenty-first century, that my parents' decision to remove my foreskin as a health precaution also fulfills part of an agreement made in the desert of Canaan millennia ago. And to a certain extent our Catholicism is ritual and tradition, something done because it has been done by those who came before us. But we still do it, still deem it important enough to practice, despite the anti-circumcision movements that argue that the practice is nothing more than mutilation, nothing more than the denial of full sexual pleasure to generations of young men, despite the apologists who argue that circumcision has been superseded by baptism.

My father tells me that they did it for hygienic reasons and that a friend of his, also Catholic, wasn't circumcised until his thirties. "It creates a more streamlined model," he says, joking, but when I have seen uncircumcised men, they seem not complete, but overdone. A brief moment with a doctor and a kit and I was cut, and that cut is so old now that it seems as though it always was.

I find it interesting that circumcision is the central part of God's covenant with Abraham. Biblical commentators argue over the significance of this; some think that it demonstrates Abraham and his followers' willingness to obey God in all things, or that it symbolizes the cutting off of the old ways. It might symbolize the cutting off with which God threatens those who break the covenant, or it might be, like the injunctions against eating shellfish, a health precaution to ensure the survival of the Jews in the desert.

But the most attractive reason hypothesizes that circumcision serves as a point of no return for Abraham and his followers, that it marks them as such in an inescapable way. In the movie *Europa*

Europa, a young Jewish man hiding as a Hitler Youth ties down the flesh of his penis in an attempt to recreate his foreskin, but his subterfuge fails when the string causes an infection. The scar of circumcision is commitment, but it is also advertisement: *This is who I am. This is where I come from. These are my people.*

The scar is the history of the self, written on the body.

The Path

Now Thomas (called Didymus), one of the Twelve, was not with the disciples when Jesus came. So the other disciples told him, "We have seen the Lord!" But he said to them, "Unless I can see the nail marks in his hands and put my finger where the nails were, and put my hand into his side, I will not believe it."

John 20:24–25, N.I.V.

I am a Midwesterner, Kansas City born, and despite living in a half dozen other states in my life, it is that city, split unevenly between Kansas and Missouri, to which I feel most closely bound. I was born in the old St. Mary's Hospital in downtown Kansas City, in the shadow of the Liberty Memorial, and my parents moved me across the state line the next day to our home in Mission, Kansas, one of the numerous suburbs that spill out from the city.

It is Kansas City where my family circled around during my childhood, moving away for a few years at a stretch, only to return each time, like homing pigeons; Kansas City where I went to school, where I was baptized and confirmed in the same church thirteen years apart, where I had my first kiss and my first heartbreak; Kansas City where I risk nostalgia, risk ignoring the bad, the racial divide of Troost Avenue, the cemetery there holding my mother's family; Kansas City where I left twelve years ago, returning only as a visitor, my family moving out west while I was in college, leaving only a few relatives—a second cousin here, a great-aunt there, a grandmother beyond the town's southern border—to remain.

I once met my roommate from college—another native—at a restaurant on 39th Street when I came into town for a visit. We caught up, he newly married and I newly moved to yet another state, over sandwiches piled thick with meat. As we stepped outside into a Midwestern evening pitched perfectly between the humid summer and the frozen winter, he looked up at the sky and said, "This town always feels like it's just about to be cool."

This is my hometown, poised on the edge of something without ever going there, constantly on the border, spilling over. And now I've returned, as has my family—mother and father, sister, grandmother and aunt and uncle, second cousins and first cousins once removed, great-uncles and aunts—all of us returning to the city of our birth for a family reunion one weekend in May, just as the schools let out and the temperature begins to rise, pushing the mercury and the humidity to unbearable levels.

* * *

My middle name is Thomas, after my father. But there are others named Thomas—Thomas Beckett, Thomas Kempis, Thomas Aquinas, and *the* Thomas, Doubting Thomas, the one who did not believe on faith alone and had to face the resurrected Christ's chastising tongue: *Blessed are those who have not seen and yet have believed.*

I was born in Missouri, the Show-Me State, a motto that, until an awful blue-green combination that made it look like a coastal state's replaced it, was stamped onto every license plate. Our motto, our identity, struck upon us by a congressman's loud declaration of doubt and identity on the floor of the state legislature. Another pathway for my requiring the empirical proof.

These things might be uniquely Midwestern—this doubt, this need for proof, this need to have the money in hand before celebrating, this *Let's wait until we get the rain before we count the crops* mentality that my farming forefathers had.

If the Midwest has a slogan, it's this, uttered everywhere every time it rains: *We really needed this.* As though we could not believe that the clouds on the horizon held anything besides expectations that would not be met, as though relief came only upon delivery of proof.

And this obsessive need of mine to see things, to see where it happened and where they are buried and where the actual bullet struck, to be, as the roadside marker always says, *On this site,* to step into history's long shadow and set up my own memory in front of the public memory. Is this not foretold in what I am called (Thomas, called Didymus) and where I am from (I am a Missourian, sir, and you must *show me!*)?

* * *

All I want is to prove that this happened.

By "this," I mean the Kansas City Massacre, the June 17, 1933, ambush by several gangsters, including Pretty Boy Floyd, in an attempt to spring Frank Nash, who was being escorted by FBI agents. Outside of Union Station the gangsters opened fire, killing not only four agents but also killing Nash. Ever since, the FBI has allowed its agents to carry firearms.

I heard this story during my childhood every time we went to downtown Kansas City, told by one parent or another. Union Station was empty those years except for a few Amtrak trains that ran through it. Politicians frequently campaigned on platforms of doing something with the building, but nothing happened.

My parents ended the story by mentioning that there were still bullet holes in the façade of the building, and as we drove by, I would press my nose to the window, trying to see, like a pilgrim looking at a saint's bone, the proof of what had happened. What's left is broken, the pieces of something destroyed and scattered.

* * *

When I return to Kansas City, I feel like nothing has changed and like everything has changed. The people who bought our house have built an extension. My high school has a multimedia lab and a library with an atrium instead of the thinly stocked shelves from which I stole books I believed no one used. Plenty of stores have gone out of business or moved elsewhere, and more have stayed in the same spot, selling the same things.

I have not expected a fly trapped in amber, and I have not expected a reinvention. What I have is a palimpsest, a city I navigate by remembering where everything once was.

Union Station, remodeled years ago, now houses a science museum, restaurant, and IMAX theater. The gift shop sells reproductions of antique postcards, which tourists can then mail from the postal service station. The giant clock that hangs from the ceiling ("meet me under the clock" was a common saying in Kansas City in the 1930s) has been refurbished and now keeps perfect time.

I'm standing underneath it right now, amazed. I am in Kansas City—I am less than half a mile from the hospital where I was born and named—but I am not in Kansas City. I'm in a recreated Kansas City, a Kansas City of my grandmother's time, of rumble seats and zoot suits and dances. I'm in a Kansas City of a time that actually traveled by train. It seems—it is?—unreal, a simulacrum of history more than history itself, something like Colonial Williamsburg, both history and not history.

Outside, I can see the elevated walkway snaking around the complex of shops and hotels. So much of my history is here: the ice skating rink (scene of awkward romantic advances); the place where golden oldies played the summer concert series (I saw Roy Orbison here not long before he died); the Irish goods shop where my mother worked part-time; the children's theater, site of field trips and an awful musical version of *Animal Farm.*

Looking down the front of the building, I try to guess where the bullet holes are, but the front of the building is large. I come to a plaque commemorating FBI agents killed in the line of duty. I can't find anything that specifically mentions the Kansas City

Massacre, but as I look at the wall next to the plaque, I find, about two feet above my head, a round divot in the marble of the building.

I reach up and fit the tip of my index finger into the hole, connected at last to a story I'd heard dozens of times. *Who shot this bullet?* I wonder, imagining the chaos as the bullets flew. When I was young, gangsters like Lester "Pretty Boy" Floyd and George "Baby Face" Nelson (Thomas, called Didymus) seemed as mythical as Robin Hood or Aladdin, but here I am now, in front of proof that Pretty Boy Floyd was real, that he tried to spring a colleague but killed him instead.

* * *

I met a Holocaust survivor this spring, a man who spent three years hiding in a pit underneath a pig trough while the rest of his village was deported to extermination camps. He told me a story about traveling recently to Belzec, the site of one of the smaller death camps, lesser known not because it was less lethal—about two hundred thousand people were killed there—but because only two or three people survived to tell about it.

He arrived at the village and began asking villagers where the site of the camp was.

"There was no camp," they told him. "Nothing happened here. Go away."

But something had happened there. I've seen photos of the Belzec site, and even though the Nazis demolished the buildings of the camp, large fragments of bones, still recognizable as femurs or scapulae, still cover the site. Something happened there, and the site itself is proof.

Union Station is the same way, albeit on a vastly smaller scale. No matter how ignored the building was, no matter how vacant it stood, no matter how far into the mists of film history *The FBI Story* vanished, the building always offered proof of its history to those who were willing to seek it out, those who were willing to believe that the proof would be there, devoutly doubting until the moment of revelation.

* * *

While I'm walking around Union Station looking for proof, my family is assembling in hotel rooms south of here, over on the Kansas side of the city, in the suburbs where those who remained live. Tonight we'll gather at a barbecue restaurant for the reunion itself, and my family's history—my history—will be available to me.

They are coming from Oklahoma and Louisiana, from Colorado and Alabama, from Texas and Kansas and Missouri, following the paths back to the place we share in common like forensic scientists tracing a bullet back from the point of impact to the barrel of the gun that fired it.

* * *

All I want is to prove that this happened.

By "this" I mean the 1981 collapse of two walkways in the lobby of the Hyatt Regency Hotel in Kansas City, which killed 114 people and injured 200 more, until the collapse of the World Trade Center the deadliest structural collapse in the United States. The accident made the front page of every newspaper in the country—the *Kansas City Star* won a Pulitzer Prize for its coverage—and is still taught in introductory engineering courses alongside the Tacoma Narrows bridge ripping itself apart in a small windstorm and the pins of a DC-10 disintegrating during takeoff in Chicago.

What happened was this: during construction, someone changed the method of how the two walkways would be suspended, one above the other. Instead of both connecting to the same support rod that descended from the ceiling (which would have required remarkably long rods), the ceiling rods held up only the first walkway, threaded through support beams. Then another set of rods, starting a few inches away from where the ceiling rods ended, descended downward to the second walkway. This allowed the walkways to be built and suspended without the abnormally long rods.

The accident also had the effect of changing the way the load of the walkways was distributed. In his book *To Engineer Is Human*, Henry Petroski describes the initial design as "two people hanging separately, one below the other, onto the same rope." As long as the rope was strong enough and each person's grip firm enough, Petroski argues, all was well. "If, however," he writes, "the lower rope-hanger grabs not the same rope but another tied to the legs of the person above, the upper person's grip must support two bodies, or roughly twice his own weight."

This is what happened to the Hyatt Regency's walkways: the upper person let go. Engineers overdesign their projects, building in alternate load pathways. If one support fails, then the load follows the path onto the other supports, at least long enough to evacuate everyone (think of all the unused bags of blood donated just after 9/11, which turned out to be unnecessary because the building held long enough for everyone below the impact sites to get out; with a few exceptions, people either made it out uninjured or died).

But when the first support gave way in Kansas City, in the Hyatt Regency during a dance, all the alternate load pathways turned into dead ends. Nowhere to go.

One hundred fourteen people dead, and half of the city, they said, connected somehow, invisible pins linking us all. Even my family, off on one of our periodic flights away from the city, found ourselves bound to a cousin who should have been there but decided not to go at the last minute. (And what could I prove to you about that cousin's decision? The hand of God? Luck? Fate? Vestigial psychic powers? She's a Kansan, anyway.)

* * *

The elevated walkway, like some umbilicus of Kansas City tragedy, links Union Station to one hotel, and then to the shopping center, and then to the Hyatt Regency itself, making it possible to walk from one historic site to another without ever going outside. The hotel lobby looks like, well, a hotel lobby. There's a front desk, chairs and couches and coffee tables arranged around the space, underneath the high ceiling of the atrium. A piece of art straight out of the catalog from which hotels apparently order their art hangs down, a cluster of silvery spheres forming a loose diamond. Imagine the lobby of a nice hotel designed in the 1970s and you're probably close.

From my vantage point on the mezzanine, I can see an opening about the shape of a doorway on the third-floor level, and, turning slowly in the lobby, I visually trace the path that a walkway might have taken to a similar opening opposite. I don't know how extensively the lobby was remodeled after the accident, although I do know that a third walkway was removed only a few days later for fear of a repeat incident.

There? I wonder. *Maybe to there?* I've seen no pictures of the lobby beforehand, only the shattered-glass aftermath, and trying to put the walkways back in the air is a futile effort. I don't even know if they ran parallel or perpendicular to each other, if they made an X or if one disappeared beneath the other.

I descend the stairs to the lobby floor and pass through the maze of furniture. On the far wall, near the elevators, I can see a brass plaque, so I make my way toward it. Glancing nervously at the front desk staff, I realize I'm afraid of getting caught, as though I'm trespassing on their property—who goes to a hotel in his hometown?—and I move a little bit faster, nothing suspicious, toward the marker.

It commemorates how to use the elevators. I turn around, looking for something else. Nothing by the concierge's desk. Nothing by the sculpture near the doors. Nothing near the stairs I came down. Nothing on the walls, nothing on the columns, nothing on the building.

As far as I can tell, the accident didn't happen.

* * *

I don't know what makes identity. I was born in Kansas City, but the first thing I remember happening—my sister's birth—took place in Indiana. I've lived longer outside the city than I did in it, and I doubt I'll ever move back there.

I don't know what makes a city's identity. I think of all those little Midwestern towns that do something to stand out on the highway—Brooklyn, Iowa, "City of Flags"; or Cawker City,

Kansas, home of the World's Largest Ball of Twine; Owatonna, Minnesota, which holds its Louis Sullivan–designed bank close to its heart; and Kearney, Missouri, full of Jesse James signage.

Kansas City spends a lot of time denying claims about itself: *not* a cow town, *not* a rural backwater, *not* the Wizard of Oz. Even the name itself misleads—most of Kansas City is in Missouri, something that never fails to confuse touring musicians.

Kansas City and I both self-censor, both hide some aspects of ourselves in order to push forward others more favorable. Union Station's the site of history, not tragedy; I'm an amateur historian and architectural buff, not some weirdo who skulks around places where people died in horrible ways. As far as we're concerned, we are who our plaques say we are, despite what any freshman engineering student knows. A little digging, a little research, and the story behind the structure opens up. And behind that another search begins, and another, another, another.

* * *

"I have an odd question for you," I say to the desk clerk. I know this is a bad way to start, but I feel as though I should warn him that I'm not asking for extra towels or where the pool is.

"Yes, sir?" he says.

"In the early '80s," I say, "there was an accident at one of the hotels around here—some walkways collapsed. Was it here?" That's good—it makes me sound like I'm not the obsessive, detail-oriented type who already knows that it happened here. I'm only a tourist asking a slightly morbid tourist question about the city's history, something he remembers reading about when he was a child.

"That was this hotel, sir," he replies, as though he gets this question a lot.

"Is there any sort of memorial plaque or anything like that?"

"No, sir."

"But one hundred fourteen people died, and there's no plaque? Isn't that covering up history? Isn't that denying one of the most significant things to happen in this city? I mean, a ten-minute walk through that glass snake takes you to another accidentally historic site, another tragedy, and we've managed to commemorate that. Who won't put a plaque up? The city? The Hyatt Corporation? Nobody thought to? What are you doing to my city?"

* * *

I didn't say that last part. Who I am (Thomas, called Didymus) versus who I present myself to be.

* * *

All I want is to prove that this happened:

Me. That I was born here, in a hospital that's gone now, near a train station with hidden holes and a hotel with a secret. That my family came from here, that we've returned here, that we will move out again when the reunion is over.

What could I show you to prove this? A birth certificate? Photographs? Both of them are easily faked. The history of this city, *my* history of this city, vanished, vanishing without any sort of memorial to mark it, only my vague, unreliable assertions.

* * *

The lament of Those Who Moved Away: what happened to my city? What happened to my childhood, my adolescence? Nostalgia is anti-history, anti-proof, the absence of a plaque in a hotel lobby, and a train station made into a replica of its previous self.

If Kansas City today teaches me anything, it is the difficulty of remembering, of negotiating a landmine field of history in an attempt to move forward. A city that does nothing but commemorate is a museum, its citizens guards, pacing along the corridors of the town, keeping its artifacts safe from the slowly destructive finger touches of guests.

But the city that moves on denies itself its history, insists that nothing happened when thousands of freshman engineering majors know exactly what happened. What is the balance between proof and life, between a bullet hole chipped into the front of a building and a hotel lobby emptied of its ghosts? If I took you on a tour of my city, you would see the history I had chosen long ago, the load paths I drew up to carry away the dangerous.

Maybe this is my ultimate problem: it's far easier and safer to accept the way we're supposed to approach our histories through monuments and memorials. Safer to feel a vague grief at the Vietnam Veterans Wall and a vague joy at the Saint Louis Arch. To ask for more risks the whole thing collapsing.

My skepticism demands proof, something I can touch, something I can feel underneath my fingers. And my faith, my belief, waiting upon it, arms folded across its chest, holes in its hands hidden from view, traveling along the alternate load paths, looking for a way to stand.

A for Answers

Where did these come from? This little one, this scratch, faint on my arm—what caused it? How many could I count if I spent an hour? Two hours? If I took a pen and traced each one, how long before I blacked out my body?

The cat's claws? A spark from a fire? An envelope opened the wrong way? A broken window? A broken sense of optimism?

Are they like a collision, cars piled up on the interstate? Are they like a graveyard, rows and rows of crosses? Does each have a story? Does anyone know every story?

What happens when we forget? What happens when we remember? What happens in the aftermath, when there's still glass on the highway, holes in the wall, blood on the ground? What happens when history keeps moving?

What happens in committee? What happens in the architect's office? What happens on the construction site? What happens at the dedication, one week later, two years later?

Do we remember with stone and steel? Do we remember in our minds or with our hearts? Do we remember the event, the story, or the memorial? Do we remember what happened or who it happened to?

I can only answer two questions: I was there, then. I am here, now. Time has moved along, decisions have been made. The place is fixed. We continue.

I was at that place *in tempore belli,* in a time of war. The drums were beating; words were all we had to stop it, and though they would fail, when I was at the place, words were the answer we had, the only explanation for the knife we were about to drag across our skin, creating another scar we would have no answer for.

Notes Toward Building the Memorial in Somerset County, Pennsylvania

1. Here is the site, and here are the names of the people who died.

2. But to reach the site—it is remote, nearly inaccessible, and although the exit for the town is well marked, I still ask the Pennsylvania Turnpike tollbooth operator for directions out of town, to the site. They have printed up directions on a small flyer, and the worker peels one off and hands it to me. There are a number of turns to take. There are many ways to become lost.

3. I should stop for lunch. I have been driving since morning. Where the flyer tells me to continue straight, I turn right, heading into the town instead of going past it. I pull into the first restaurant that looks good enough.

4. Inside, the restaurant is decorated in a regional theme, like those national chain restaurants, with memorabilia and photos all over the walls. Here is the Somerset Area Senior High School pennant, here is a drawing of the town in 1850, here is a coal miner's lantern. The menu has the peculiarly Pennsylvanian meal of french fries on top of salad, which I have eaten before and which is better than it sounds. I order a Reuben.

5. To stretch my legs after driving all morning, I get up and walk around the restaurant, looking at the walls of the renovated house it occupies. One room is open, but a little dark. A man on a ladder works on one of the overhead lights. I ask him if I can look around, and he says, "Sure."

6. There is no identifying label on the photo that I find in the middle of the wall, surrounded by other artifacts of the city, but I recognize it without one, though I have never seen this photo before.

7. Here is the photo: green field, green woods, and above that a black plume of smoke that looks like a balloon let go into the sky.

8. "That vanished after about ten minutes," says the man on the ladder. "I heard a boom, so I ran outside and saw that smoke rising up from the property next to ours. I grabbed my camera and took that picture. We jumped in the car and drove over there as fast as we could, and got there before any of the police did. There wasn't anything there, no big pieces of the plane. I thought a little Cessna had crashed at first."

9. "Of course, later we knew it wasn't. A guy not far from here said he saw the plane pass near him, only a couple hundred feet off the ground, upside down. Probably what happened is that they were struggling for control in the cockpit, the plane rolled over, someone got ahold of the stick, and—you know how you pull back on the stick to go up?—pulled back, which sent the plane almost vertically into the ground."

10. He has made his hand into the plane, pushing it forward, turning it over, and bending it downward.

11. "We'd just had a bunch of rain, so that ground was soft, really soft. It just swallowed the plane."

12. "Later on, when the FBI guys were investigating it, they'd come here at the end of the day. I'd close the restaurant and just let them have whatever they wanted. They'd come here and cry and get angry and try to get ready for the next day, and I tried to give them a place where they could do it without anyone else around."

13. He has stayed on the ladder the whole time. Those were the days when no one seemed to have any idea of what was going on. Days of rumors and urgings to be vigilant. Days when the story from here, from everywhere, seemed to trickle out and we tried to fill it in as best we could with the story we wanted to hear.

14. This site is in Somerset County, Pennsylvania, near Shanksville, and it is early March 2003. It seems important to come here now, as war seems an inevitability again and there are a dozen

sides to take, and it seems important to come here, to the last place where anything in this country felt simply binary: right and wrong, good and evil. I came here because I felt like I should see the site before they decide what to build on it, before the committees and architects and politicians have their way with it. I want to see it before the scar heals over.

15. I return to my table and eat my Reuben, which is good but not great, and part of me wishes I had ordered the french fry/salad thing, because I don't know when I'll be back in Pennsylvania. I leave the restaurant. The ladder stands in an empty room.

16. The directions from the tollbooth operator are complicated but clear, and though I have to drive a long way out of town to the site, I never get lost. There are many places where I *feel* lost, but then I drive a little more and realize that I am on the right path. All the way, I am trying to mesh what I see through my windshield to the one image I remember from three days of nonstop news coverage: a group of police, or maybe firefighters, or maybe rescue workers combing the site, a furrow of ground still smoking. Then:

17. Here is the site, and here are the names of the people who died.

18. The monument is chain-link fence and some bracing poles put together to make a wall, maybe twenty feet long by ten feet high, and the wall is covered with tributes from people who have driven here to see the site. It stands on the side of a gravel parking lot. If I turn ninety degrees to my left and look toward the trees

about one hundred yards from where I am, I will see a fence with an American flag on it. Beyond that fence is where the plane sank into the ground.

19. It is good that they have separated us, the visitors, from the actual site, because I have heard that even now, over a year later, if I were to walk on the crash site and brush the snow and ice off the grass, I would still find bits of broken circuitry and lengths of wire. Most people come here to leave something in tribute, but I believe that many of them would take something if they could, too. I am trying very hard not to harbor any illusions about the world these days. Every time I turn on the radio, I hear talk of necessary war.

20. Back in the parking lot and memorial area, there is a ranger huddled against the wind. I have not mentioned the wind yet. The wind astonishes me with its force. The other people in the parking lot and I have to lean into the wind and hold our hats on our heads simply to walk up to the wall. The highest things out here, higher than the memorial wall, are two flagpoles: one with the American flag, the other with the blue Pennsylvania flag. The wind pulls at these two flags so hard that they have begun to fray at the edges, and I can see loose threads flickering in the storm.

21. When I ask the ranger about them, she tells me that this set of flags was first raised three days ago. Depending on the wind, she tells me, they go through two or three sets a week. She holds a binder and opens it up to show me photos of the site that day. There is the photo I remember from the news, and there is the photo of the smoke, the one I saw hanging in the restaurant.

22. The ranger is not a ranger—she is a volunteer. After all, this is still private land, though some day it will be purchased or annexed by the federal government, and whoever is in charge of these things (the National Park Service? the Department of the Interior?) will take down this temporary wall and build a permanent memorial here.

23. For now there is just the wall, and it is covered with the remembrances of all the people who come here. The wall is made of these objects that people have brought from all over to leave here, so that they might mark their visit and say they remembered this place and those who died here and what they died for. I cannot discern any pattern to what people leave here. Some things—dozens of small American flags, for example—make perfect sense, but so many of the objects left here bear no direct relationship to what happened.

24. People have pinned caps to the wall, some from a group—American Legion, Pittsburgh Chapter—some from a team. There is a license plate: Illinois D 319 341, a dealer plate. And another, a blue vanity plate: USA4ME.

25. Posters on the wall, including a large white one on which it seems like a thousand people have signed their names. The Somerset County Vietnam Veterans Association has put up a sign that says "We Understand." A painting of a bald eagle. A girl has left her school ID card tucked into the links of the fence. Her face looks out over the road that leads here.

26. Some objects are too big to fit on the fence, so they sit at its base, where the wind blows the snow onto them. Some are half buried in ice, the tops of them emerging out of the cold like headlights out of the fog. Artificial flowers, orchids crusted with ice. A T-shirt from Ohio. A baseball player bobblehead, its head shaking in the wind. A block of wood, painted in red, white, and blue, that says "God Bless" and has a white dog with red and blue stars on it. On the side of the box are three painted smiley faces, red and white, white and blue, blue and red.

27. People bring things here every day. The volunteer ranger tells me that already the Somerset County Historical Society has placed thousands of items in storage and thrown away thousands of pounds of flowers. It is possible that someday these items might be displayed in a museum—that is, if a museum is in the plans for whatever will be built here.

28. Because something will be built here. An event of this magnitude, a loss of this caliber could not occur in this country without a memorial eventually constructed to mark it.

29. And what form should it take? I cannot imagine that an eternal flame would last very long out here in a wind that tears a flag apart in three days.

30. If the government were to install a realistic sculpture on the site—one like, say, the Iwo Jima memorial in DC—what would it be? Passengers storming up the aisle, fists raised, a terrorist cowering when faced with American spirit? Bronze busts of the dead?

31. A plane flying upside down before it curves sharply downward?

32. All of these ideas would bring too-concrete images to visitors' minds, make the death too real, overshadow the heroism with tragedy. And what, after all, does a monument do but usurp tragedy?

33. The obelisks of the war dead—what do they do but give heroes the glorious repose we deem they deserve? They overshadow the immediate cause of death—the bullet, the cannonball, the poison gas—with the cause for which they died.

34. Everyone calls the passengers on this plane heroes. The phrase one of them spoke—*Let's roll*—I see it on bumper stickers now. The widow of one of the dead sits at the president's right hand as he makes a speech.

35. (But wait! We don't know what happened on the plane for sure. The flight recorder ends with shouting, both in English and in Arabic, but the question of whether the passengers breached the cabin door remains a mystery.)

36. Whoever builds this monument must avoid the eternal flame, the realist sculpture, the obelisk of heroes. They must be abstract but specific. What they will build here, I imagine, will be another wall, stone or maybe steel, with the names engraved into it. Abstract but not anonymous. Ten years from now, you will come here, and:

37. Here is the site, and here are the names of the people who died.

38. (But, of course, not all forty-four names of those who died on the plane. There are four of them best forgotten, the four with box cutters and first-class tickets.)

39. So they will probably build a wall and remove the wall that stands there now, and though people will still leave mementoes at the new wall, the new wall will not be composed of these left-behind memories, for what is a memento but a memory made manifest, and who does the remembering for one when it is left at a memorial?

40. The wall will list the names, and the names will be the same as the names on the snow-buried wooden angels that someone has painted with stars and stripes and left planted along the edge of the field. Around the neck of the angel of one of the flight attendants someone has hung a luggage tag that reads "crew," and at the base of the angel of the man who said "Let's roll" other people have left tokens, more than at the bases of other angels. I wish I could leave something behind here, something that might be in a museum someday.

41. Manifest (noun): a list of the names of the passengers and crew of an aircraft. Manifest (verb): to make something certain by showing or displaying. Manifest (adjective): easily understood or recognized by the mind: *a manifest truth.*

42. When they build the monument here, it will lose the spontaneity of this temporary wall. It will lose this nearly frantic desire to leave something, anything that the people who come here feel, that I feel right now. It will lose the direct honesty of a cap and a license plate and even a painted dog with blue and red stars. The new wall will only say:

43. Here is the site, and here are the names of the people who died.

44. What will be lost? What will be saved?

A for Anatomy

I remember, during my training as an altar boy, the priest rolling up the cloth that normally covered the marble altar of our church, Saint Agnes, to reveal a square plug of white stone.

"Under this," he said, "is our saint's relic. A piece of bone."

My eyes must have widened. At that age I was obsessed with saints and the stories of their gruesome martyrdoms, of bodily sacrifice for the glory of God. Even during college and a few years after, when I was convinced of my agnosticism, I still found the lives of the saints irresistible to contemplate, their devotion and belief a contrast to my own twenty-something disaffected world-weariness.

The body plays a central role in Catholicism; one of Martin Luther's main objections was to the doctrine of transubstantiation, which holds that at the moment of consecration the bread and wine literally—not a metaphor, not poetic license, but literally—become the body and blood of Christ.

The lives of the saints are full of examples of holy men and women who lived on nothing but the Eucharist and who, when they died, left behind bodies preserved from decay through the power of God. Their bodies, corpses inviolate, lay in repose as monuments to an all-powerful God, a God who could make even transitory flesh as lasting as stone, who could turn scars to lines etched in marble. Even now, in Saint Peter's Basilica, the preserved body of Pope John XXIII is visible to pilgrims and tourists alike, although the Vatican ascribes the state of the body to embalming and a carefully sealed coffin.

Standing in front of the altar years ago, staring wide-eyed at a block of stone, I had no way of knowing that I would spend almost ten years not believing in God, or that I would eventually come back to believing. All I knew at that moment was the power of the body to speak, to testify, to hold sway over those who saw it.

"I believe in the resurrection of the body," we say in the Apostles' Creed, our statement of belief. Each Catholic church has some sort of saint's relic, a bone shard or scrap of cloth once worn, that sanctifies the edifice and makes it holy.

When Nazi Germany began its collection of other countries, first through annexation and then through invasion, hundreds of churches, fearing the worst, shipped their relics to safe places. And when the worst came, those churches were destroyed and members killed, either on the battlefield or in a concentration camp, through starvation or through execution.

The relics survived, sometimes the only proof that the church they'd come from had ever existed. Hundreds of them reside where they were initially sent, at the Maria Stein Center in Ohio, just east of the Indiana state line. The church has become a site of pilgrimage for Catholics, both in the Midwest and outside, because the relics have survived when others did not. It is the martyrs—Saint Agnes, the victims of war, the relics without a home—that we honor most.

World War II gave us the greatest scar of our long history, even by the hyper-memorializing standards of the twentieth century. In the decades since the liberation of the Nazi concentration camps, we have struggled with how to remember the Holocaust, the extermination of European Jews by Nazi Germany and its allies. Even the name we call it provokes controversy: "*holocaust*" is a Greek word meaning "sacrifice," something burned to curry favor with God. More appropriate, then, is the Hebrew *shoah,* which means simply "annihilation."

But even "annihilation" isn't completely accurate. History remains at the sites, memory resides there in the form of the memorial, our physical commemoration of those who died because of who they were, and who remain there in bits and pieces of ash smaller than the relic over which I wondered as a child.

Victims

THE YELLOW FLOWERS

/10:00/Warsaw Central Station

Here's how it happened: the locomotive picked up twenty cars and took them to the camp. That took maybe an hour.

Underground. Double-checking my train's departure time on the encased poster, I pass a note to the ticket agent. I do not speak Polish, nothing beyond a weak *Do you speak English?* and so all of my communication in this country is written out, copied carefully from my phrase book.

She looks at my note, crosses out the part where I have written *miejscówka;* evidently, there are no reservations on the train to Bialystok. She writes a number on the sheet and pushes it back under, and I, acting out the agreed-upon choreography of all retail transactions, hand her thirty *zloty,* a little under ten dollars.

Walking away, I roll my change in my hand, a five-zloty coin, enough for breakfast. My train ticket, *Warszawa Centralna-Małkinia,* rests in my bag, next to my camera, next to my guidebook, next to my notebook. My feet are covered in blisters from the last three days of walking around Warsaw; one, on my left heel, looks like a fat slug has taken up residence. It will be nice to sit down for a while.

/10:30/Warsaw→Małkinia

I was together with them. I know in my heart that something is not good,
because if they take children, if they take old people, they send them away,
that means it is not good. What they said is they take them away to
a place where they will be working. But on the other hand, an old woman,
a little child of four weeks or five years, what is work? It was a foolish
thing, but still, we had no choice—we believed in them.

If there are other people in my compartment, I don't see them. Men stand at the windows of the train's passageway and blow smoke into the Polish countryside. Farms rush past us, fields starting to grow to noticeable heights at the very end of May. The sun shines brilliantly upon them.

I thumb through my guidebook again, though I have read the slim paragraph on Treblinka too many times already, enough to have memorized its advice. *Not many tourists visit Treblinka,* I repeat to myself, *which only adds to the poignancy of the site.*

I'm here for a few weeks, touring around Poland. I'm a Catholic—I even went to mass yesterday at the Church of the Holy Cross in Warsaw, where Chopin's heart is buried (another site checked off in the guidebook). But I am drawn to Treblinka for a number of reasons: guilt, curiosity, the desire to see how the biggest murder of all time is memorialized. Back in college, I saw Claude Lanzmann's massive documentary *Shoah,* and I still remember his camera moving through the Polish forest to come upon the Treblinka site. And so I am on a train.

The guidebook suggests what sounds to me like a complicated route, involving a train, a bus, and a walk along a Polish highway. I focus instead on the entry's last line: *alternatively, go to Małkinia and negotiate a taxi.*

Yes. Of course. I turn to the appropriate page in my phrase book and write, on another sheet of paper, "I would like to go to the Treblinka camp. How much will it cost?"

/11:00/Warsaw→Małkinia

There was a sign, a small sign, on the station of Treblinka. I don't know if
we were at the station or if we didn't go up to the station. On the line
over there where we stayed there was a sign, a very small sign, which
said "Treblinka." That was the first time in my life I heard that name
"Treblinka." Because nobody knew.

The train shakes on the tracks. I sit in the sun, starting to sweat. *What is Treblinka?* I wonder. *What was Treblinka?*

An easy recitation of facts: eight hundred thousand dead, brought by trains from as far away as France and Greece, as close as the next town over. In 1942 the Warsaw Ghetto was liquidated, its three hundred thousand inhabitants sent to die in the gas chambers of Treblinka, rooms hooked up to tank engines that pumped in the carbon monoxide. Its momentary prisoners' revolt, combined with the opening of more efficient gas chambers at Auschwitz-Birkenau to the south, led to the closing of Treblinka in 1943, to its erasure from the field, the demolition of all the bunkers and buildings, the incineration of every corpse.

Beyond that, there aren't many facts about Treblinka. Although it was the second-most lethal camp, it lacks all the evidence Auschwitz provides. No remaining crematoriums, no barracks, no ash ponds to sift through. No dozens of informative signs dotting its landscape, telling visitors what happened, what the function of this building was, where to go next.

Auschwitz remains the best-known camp because of the thousands of survivors who walked out of it alive, because of the evidence abandoned by the Germans in the face of the advancing Red Army. Those piles of shoes and eyeglasses, those piles of hair.

Eight hundred thousand people died, and at the later trials of the officers, only fifty-four survivors of Treblinka were left to testify. Add the Germans who worked there and the Poles who lived nearby, and perhaps only one hundred people existed who could have still told us about this place where seventy years ago the flames reached into the sky.

Auschwitz is history, proof. Treblinka is memory, projections at best.

/11:30/Małkinia Station

Then, on the second day, I saw a sign for Małkinia. We went on a little farther. Then, very slowly, the train turned off of the main track and rolled at a walking pace through a wood. While he looked out—we'd been able to open a window— the old man in our compartment saw a boy . . . cows were grazing . . . and he asked the boy in signs, "Where are we?" And the kid made a funny gesture. This: (draws finger across his throat).

With the few other people disembarked here at Małkinia already dispersed, I'm at a loss for what to do. I'm prepared to negotiate a taxi, but there are none to be seen. I walk around, enter the little snack shop by the station, look around, walk back out. I walk to the road, look down both ways. I don't even know which way I should walk.

I sit on the bench at the empty taxi stand, and as I retie my shoes, trying to relieve the pressure on my blisters, a taxi pulls up. I take the slip of paper out of my pocket, read it over, think maybe I could give the Polish a try. Before I can do so, the driver, a man in his sixties, looks at me and says simply, "Treblinka?"

"Yes," I say, standing up and shrugging on my backpack. Then, remembering my little Polish, I add, "*Tak.*"

We do not negotiate. I want too badly to see the site, have already come an hour and a half and one hundred kilometers from Warsaw to see it. I get in the car.

/11:40/Treblinka village

At that time we started working in that place they called Treblinka. Still
I couldn't believe what had happened over there on the other side of
the gate, where the people went in, everything disappeared, and everything
got quiet.

Treblinka is a town. Treblinka was a death camp. Treblinka is a monument.

The taxi speeds along roads, around bicyclists and other cars, past fields. I never would have been able to negotiate the necessary turns. We speed through Treblinka, the village from which the camp took its name, and over the Bug River.

The taxi driver turns to me, and asks, "America? New York?"

"America, *tak,*" I say. "New York, *nie*—Alabama." I add a little rise to my voice at the end, questioning if he's heard of the state. If he has, I can't tell. We continue the drive and soon reach the site's parking lot. After some odd gesturing and a bit more scribbling on scraps of paper, we agree that he will return in two and a half hours to pick me up and return me to the station for the last train to Warsaw.

I pay him, and with a wave he drives off. Looking around the parking lot, I note not a single car. The only other person here is manning the information kiosk. I walk up to her, buy a map of the site, and set off into the trees that have grown back in the last seven decades.

Near here are forests and wetlands, untouched by man. Bison roam, the guidebook says. I am in the last wilderness of Europe. I am by myself.

/11:45/Treblinka II

We couldn't ask what had happened to the wife, to the kid. "What do you mean—wife, kid? Nobody is anymore!" How could they kill, how could they gas so many people at once? But they had a way to do it.

Treblinka is dual. The first camp, Treblinka I, served mainly as a labor camp in which Polish prisoners worked; about ten thousand of them died there. Treblinka II is the better-known site, the execution camp, location of the gas chambers and the endless fires and the false train station, complete with a fake clock whose hands were pushed to the right time just before a transport came in.

Postwar, the road to Treblinka from Warsaw took five hours to travel, through small villages and along dirt roads. People rarely visited the site—too awful to see the bones and skulls that still lay among the trees and fields planted by the perpetrators. For fourteen years the site stayed empty, mostly unvisited. Poland struggled with its own sense of martyrology, its own loss, its own six million.

In 1957 the site was set aside, preserved for its monument, and on February 28, 1960, the Warsaw Regional Council accepted a design by sculptor Adam Haupt and architect Franciszek Duszeńko. It aimed to recreate the camp symbolically, using very few words and no plaques. Fitting Treblinka's status as a massive graveyard, they chose to finally give the site its tombstones.

Forty-five years later I stand at the reconstructed gates of Treblinka, about to enter. Haupt and Duszeńko have set two granite walls at an angle, leaving a gap between the two, a stylized map of the camp's trapezoidal shape carved into one of them.

I could enter here, but it seems wrong, or worse than wrong. Very few of the camp's victims arrived on foot or drove in through this gate. They came by train.

I turn around and walk back to the road that leads to Treblinka I and follow it for a short while before encountering the designers' recreation of the railway line that once led into camp: a series of concrete ties, running parallel to each other, that lead out of the woods. Looking forward, I can see a flat concrete platform, the symbolic sorting ramp where the guards pulled out the few prisoners who would not be killed immediately and told the others to undress for disinfection. Nearby, a series of tall stones loom, perhaps fifty meters between each one, marking the outline of the camp's boundaries.

The site of an atrocity—no matter how much preparation and research one might do before going there, no matter how many survivors' testimonies one reads, no matter how many films and books one absorb—still holds a power to shock. Standing next to the first concrete tie, I realize: *I'm here. This place is real. The things that happened actually had a place where they happened.*

I'm here, and I'm alone. I'm the only living person in a massive cemetery.

I start walking toward the ramp.

/11:50/Treblinka II

Clothes, suitcases, everything stacked in a solid mass. On top of it, jumping around like demons, people were making bundles and carrying them outside. I was turned over to one of these men. His armband said "Squad Leader." He shouted, and I understood that I was also to pick up clothing, bundle it, and take it somewhere. As I worked, I asked him: "What's going on? Where are the ones who stripped?" And he replied: "Dead! All dead!"

My eyes are closed. I can feel the sun warm my skin. Whenever I have thought about visiting Treblinka or any of the camps—and I have thought of this often since I was a child—I have imagined the weather as overcast and gloomy, the gray of ashes.

Here, though, the day is wonderful. I can hear birds singing in the trees, and I know if I open my eyes, I will see a blue sky with no clouds, green trees, and fields filled with little yellow flowers, their blooms no bigger than my thumbnail.

And if I open my eyes, I will also see the central monument of Treblinka: an eight-meter-high granite obelisk with a wide cap, split from top to bottom, surrounded by seventeen thousand shards of granite set into a concrete field. Haupt and Duszeńko's design, named by historian James Young as "perhaps the most magnificent of Holocaust memorials," will spread before me. All I have to do is open my eyes.

I have imagined this for so long, have seen dozens of still photos of it, stared at it in Lanzmann's documentary. I already know what it looks like. But to open my eyes, to make it real, to experience the memorial that will confirm the camp's reality, is turning out to be harder than I think.

Finally, I open my eyes. And there it is.

I have to confess it's smaller than I thought.

/12:15/Treblinka II

But it still hadn't sunk in, I didn't

believe it.

Snapping photos while wandering among the shards, I try to record what I see, hoping I'll be able to link memory to image later. Some of the shards are small enough to trip over, so I have to look down as I walk about, and each time I look up, I'm overwhelmed by how many stones I can see.

In memorializing something on the scale of the Holocaust, any design team will confront the problem of scale—after a while, numbers of victims simply become numbers, abstract, meaningless; it's easy to say "six million." How, then, to illustrate the scope of such tragedy while maintaining the individuality of each victim?

Yad Vashem, the museum and memorial in Jerusalem, undertook a project not long after its conception in 1953 to record the individual names and biographies of each Jew murdered in the Holocaust, resulting in the museum's Hall of Names, a library-monument. This makes sense; after all, Israel was the site where the Jewish people were able to reestablish their identity after the destruction of their communities in Europe, where even the cemeteries were destroyed and the tombstones scraped clean from the earth.

Treblinka is different. At Treblinka the victims moved anonymously, stripped of their clothes, from the sorting ramp, along the curved path (called the *Himmelweg,* the Road to Heaven) to the gas chambers. The women's heads were shaved, their hair shipped out from the camp to be used in industry. They were made anonymous, and they were killed as anonymous people.

To signal the start of the gas, a guard would yell, *"Iwan, wasser!"* At the camp's peak efficiency, seventeen thousand people heard this each day, the last thing they heard before the screams and panic overtook everything. Seventeen thousand.

Now there are seventeen thousand stones set into the concrete, surrounding the obelisk at the site of the gas chambers, surrounding the black metal that symbolizes the open pit where the bodies were burned. Seventeen thousand stones, each different, but each as unknowable as the sound of the door shutting upon the gas chamber must have sounded.

Some stones have the names of cities on them, cities from which Jews arrived. The Warszawa stone is the largest, but as I walk around, I see the names of other cities: Częstochowa, Małkinia. Many of the stones have smaller stones and pebbles balanced on them, as is often done in Jewish cemeteries to signify a visitor has paid homage. Appropriately so: I am at one of the largest cemeteries on earth, and each stone that juts out of the ground stands for so many dead. Even the yellow flowers that grow here are a memorial, sown by the perpetrators as a cover for the ash-choked earth. Every spring they bloom, a quiet remembrance emerging from the ground, as fragile as the shards are permanent, as anonymous as the dead are known. As countless.

/13:15/Along the Black Road

> At night we were put into a barracks. It just had a sand floor. Nothing else. Each of us simply dropped where he stood. Half asleep, I heard some men hang themselves. We didn't react then. It was almost normal.

Other sites await at Treblinka, so I set off down the Black Road that connects the two camps, so named by the prisoners of Treblinka I because of the awful labor they once performed, quarrying gravel from a pit.

Two kilometers stretch between the camps, and soon enough I leave behind the boundary stones to walk along a bumpy road. After a while I encounter a small, tent-shaped structure, concrete, near the woods. My map tells me this building is a guard bunker, yet there are no signs or explanations on site.

I look through the small window of the bunker at the Black Road. This is as close as anything comes to reconstruction at Treblinka, this small window offering a single point of view of a small section of road. Haupt and Duszeńko's memorial allows for visitors to project themselves upon it, to understand the seventeen thousand as graves, as markers, as stone flowers growing from concrete ground. The bunker is simply a bunker.

/13:30/Treblinka I

> There was Death, had to be Death, for no one was supposed to be left to bear witness. I already knew that, three hours after arriving at Treblinka.

The monument at Treblinka I, built around the same time as Treblinka II's, is a red stone marker with a cross rising behind it. From that central monument, rows of smaller crosses extend out in three directions.

Something happens at Treblinka I that seems almost impossible at Treblinka II: the victims are named. Not all—there aren't ten thousand crosses here, not even one thousand—but most crosses have a name, dates, sometimes even a photo on them.

Close to the monument stand the foundations of the buildings of Treblinka I—the barracks and the bunkers, the warehouses, the guards' swimming pool. They have decayed—the walls of the root cellar are propped up with wooden beams, and plants grow furiously through cracks in its bricks—but they are nevertheless there.

Treblinka I is specific, offering the possibility of understanding through reconstruction. Ultimately, its monument is redundant. As at Auschwitz, there's no need for a monument here to focus memory; the site does so by itself.

Only where erasure has taken place does memorializing become necessary.

I look at my watch; time is slipping away. I need to return the way I came, to do the impossible and leave Treblinka.

/14:00/Treblinka II

There were also cases of children who for some reason arrived alone, or got separated from their parents. These children were led to the "infirmary" and shot there.

But first there remains one contradiction: the Janusz Korczak stone.

Added in 1978 on the centenary of his birth, the stone commemorates the head of the orphanage of the Warsaw Ghetto who chose to accompany his charges to Treblinka despite an opportunity to avoid deportation. He is remembered everywhere as one of the heroes/martyrs of the Holocaust: in memorials in the Jewish cemetery in Warsaw, in front of his orphanage, even in a memorial at Yad Vashem, thousands of miles distant.

His name is the only one spoken at the Treblinka II site, the only person remembered out of eight hundred thousand, the only name out of the seventeen thousand who died on that particular day.

Korczak's stone is as covered with pebbles as the Warsaw stone. Candles sprout at the base; dozens brought here and lit beside the piles of flowers left each year on the anniversary of his deportation. He is the first individual I have thought about in the entire time I have been here, an exception to the masses of anonymous stone shards.

I step up to the obelisk and run my hand along the vertical crack splitting its face in two. Looking up, I can see the twisted and tortured victims emerging from the granite cap.

I have only minutes. In all likelihood I will never return here again, so I slowly walk backward from the monument, toward the loading ramp and the concrete railroad ties. Soon I will have to go back to relying on photographs and testimonies, reels of film and rows of books. For a final moment I stand staring at the obelisk and the shards before following the concrete ties back into the woods, wondering how to make it real.

/14:15/Treblinka parking lot

It was impossible. The hollering and the crying was in your ears and your mind   for days and days, and at night the same thing. From the howling you couldn't   even sleep a couple of nights. All at once at one time everything stopped by a   command. It was all quiet.

At the lot, the cab driver is waiting. I get into the car, and he looks at me, his eyes fixed. He reaches out, pats me on the knee a few times.

"OK?" he asks.

For a moment I'm taken aback. When he asked me if I was from New York, it probably wasn't because of any generalizations about America, but because New York is home to thousands of victims, survivors, and their children and grandchildren, many of whom inevitably return here to the place where their families died. This cab driver, I realize, must pick up dozens of people who are utterly wrecked and shaken to their cores by the memorial. People who sob openly in his cab with a grief that only actually visiting the site can confer.

He has learned, I realize, that he is a custodian of memory, of remembrance, and of this site. He and the stones, and the sky, and the trees, and the yellow flowers that spring from the ground each year, are custodians to the void of Treblinka, to extermination, to the eight hundred thousand dead who still reside here, anonymous, yet not overlooked.

I nod my head a few times, then add, quietly, "*Dziekuje.*" My last bit of Polish. Thank you.

/14:30/Małkinia Station

Some of the Germans, some of the other people that were there, the Ukrainians and other ones, they start shouting and hitting us that we should do it faster, to carry the bundles to the main place where there were big piles of clothes, of shoes, of other things. And in no time this was clean as though people had never been on that place. There was no trace, none at all, like a magic thing, everything disappeared.

As my train winds its way back through the countryside toward Warsaw, I write postcards to friends back home, trying to explain myself, hoping the photo on the front of the card gives them some sense of where I stood. I scratch out a description, then add, *That sounds stupid now that I've written it.* My blisters, quiet all day, start to ache once more.

The Treblinka memorial, though nearly wordless, says far more than any explanatory text. Faced with the unspeakable horror of the Holocaust, it chooses to maintain that silence, to leave the words to the survivors and historians. To those still willing to walk and witness, the memorial gives body to the voices we hear.

I tuck my clumsy postcards inside my notebook, next to the camera, guidebook, and phrase book. Looking out the window, I watch the blossoming fields slip past, giving way slowly to more and more buildings, becoming city, until suddenly, finally, the train is shrouded in darkness as we enter the tunnel that leads to the Warsaw underground.

Bystanders

THE END OF THE WORLD

ONE: THE LITURGY OF THE WORD

I don't understand the language, but I still know what's happening.

At the altar in front of me, the priest speaks the words of greeting. The crowd responds appropriately. I hear a few words that I understand. No, not true. I hear one: *Bog.* God.

Few things in this world are quieter than a small Polish town on a Sunday. In a country where 90 percent of the populace is Catholic, just about everything shuts down, and all activity centers on the Masses that run every hour of the morning, churches packed to overflowing each time.

My stomach growls loudly, protesting the small breakfast I ate this morning at the Centrum Dialogu i Modlitwy—the Center for Dialogue and Prayer—where I've been the last four days. In response I try to remember if I saw any open restaurants when I walked across the bridge over the Soła River this morning, crossing from the outskirts of town into the center. I come up empty but promise my stomach that we'll find something after Mass ends.

I shift in the wooden pew. Normally I'd feel bad about letting my mind wander during Mass, but I know that we're in the middle of the homily, and I don't speak much Polish beyond the basic travel phrases. Still, though, it's an amazing trick of memory and tradition that I can follow the ceremony from beginning to end—from readings, to offertory, to consecration, to Eucharist. I anticipate the moments when we stand or sit, and when it comes time to exchange a sign of peace, I know, thanks to last week's Mass in Warsaw, that I should simply nod at the people around me instead of shaking their hands as Catholics do in America.

I'm often aware of my body as a Catholic: the pop of a knee as I kneel, the agonized Christ hanging from the crucifix, the stories of saints' suffering. At the moment the priest raises the bread of the Eucharist over his head it will be transformed into the body of Christ—literally the body of Christ, according to the doctrine of transubstantiation. Even though the priest's words are incomprehensible, I believe that this happens. The body matters to the Church.

I walk out with everyone, past the group of people waiting for the next service. In America, when I go to Mass I can leave my apartment five minutes before Mass starts and still get a seat. Here, however, each ceremony is packed to capacity.

The sky is overcast, the first time in days that the Polish weather hasn't been postcard-perfect. Rain seems like a distinct possibility.

I follow the street back up to the town square. There's little activity now that I'm away from the church. A mother and child walk up the sidewalk on the opposite side from me, and I can hear a few voices from a beer garden in the center, but the only restaurants open are "Pizza Hit" and a nondescript burger place.

For speed's sake, I pick the burger place, and after eating a burger on a sliced kaiser roll, with shredded carrots and peppers and some sort of white cheese melted on top—after I address my own bodily needs—I walk over to the nearby building (the city hall, I'm guessing) that occupies one entire side of the town square.

The building has a number of commemorative markers on it, including the usual ones I've seen all over Poland for Solidernošć activity in the region and the Polish Home Army during World War II. Next to the others, one plaque catches my eye, and although it's in Polish, I recognize one word: *zydów.* Jews.

I don't understand the language, but I still know what's happened.

Despite having been in the southern Polish town of Oświęcim for four days, this is the first time I have been to the town square, or over the bridge that leads to it, or anywhere else near the heart of the town. I, like most visitors to Oświęcim, have been concerned with a site at the town's edge, a site that makes Oświęcim famous not because of its reputation as "Land of the Night Heron," as one birdwatching brochure points out, but because of its role in the largest murder in history.

Each morning for the last four days, I have woken up, showered, eaten breakfast, and then walked four blocks, past open fields and houses and a roadside shrine to Saint Christopher, to arrive at Auschwitz. Along with thousands of other tourists each day, I visit the site where a million and a half people, 90 percent of them Jews, were killed in the largest and most lethal of the Nazi concentration camps.

Most people visit Auschwitz on a day trip from Kraków. They take a train in the morning, tour Auschwitz, maybe tour Birkenau (the much larger subcamp where the vast majority of gassings and murders took place), and then get on the train back to Kraków, back to their hotels or homes in time for a nice dinner. I, on the other hand, am staying at a church-run hostel, where I appear to be one of only a few guests. I'm staying here for five days, five times longer than any guidebook suggests. I have time, nothing but, to wander around, seeing everything, making it my mission to see everything.

The sky is gray, the barometric pressure falling noticeably. Stomach full, I walk away from city hall and its plaques and start moving toward the main road, the road I need to follow.

* * *

I have nothing new to say about Auschwitz. I knew this coming here on the train, that Auschwitz was simply too big, too well known, for me to produce any sort of new thought about it.

The Holocaust killed millions of Jews in numerous ways—starvation in the ghettos, the *Einsatzgruppen* mobile killing squads in the occupied Soviet Union, random killings all over, even indirectly, through suicides—but for many of us, Auschwitz simply *is* the Holocaust. Auschwitz is the gas chambers disguised as showers, the ovens, the chimneys, the barracks for fifty-two horses that instead held almost eight hundred people.

Holocaust historian Raul Hilberg argues that Auschwitz's symbolic nature comes from three factors: first, that more Jews died there than anywhere else; second, that they came from all over, from as far away as Greece and Norway, France and the USSR; and third, that the camp continued the process of annihilation long after the other killing centers—Treblinka, Sobibor, and others—had been shut down, long after it became obvious that Germany would not win the war.

Another historian, Robert Jan van Pelt, puts the case for Auschwitz's dominance of memory more lyrically. Speaking of Crematorium II in Birkenau, he says, "In the 2,500 square feet of this one room, more people lost their lives than any other place on this planet—500,000 people were killed. If you would draw a map of human suffering, if you create a geography of atrocity, this would be the absolute center."

But everyone knows this, that Auschwitz was the center of pointless mass murder. No one needs it explained the way he or she might need things like the *Einsatzgruppen* or the Aktion Reinhard camps explained. Say "Auschwitz," and the word comes preloaded with a concept. All I can offer is a catalog of what is there, of what surrounds it, of every memorial marker that dots the place.

* * *

I'm down to my last two books. I don't speak the language, and for the two weeks I've been in Poland, my conversations in English have been limited to ordering meals and checking into hostels. I'm able to read e-mail from friends and family back home only sporadically, when I can find an Internet café. I feel like I'm beginning to exist without words that I can understand, and that when I finish my last two books, I'll be lost, without any way to communicate to the people I encounter in Poland.

At breakfast I read Viktor Frankl's *Man's Search for Meaning* over my cereal and cheese and meat and coffee. Frankl spent three years as a prisoner at Auschwitz and, because he was a doctor, worked in the camp's medical ward. His book, published in 1946, is both a memoir of his experience at the camp and an explanation of his psychiatric theory of logotherapy. He writes, "Logotherapy . . . focuses on the meaning of human existence as well as man's search for such a meaning." Hence the title.

In the evenings after the camp museum closes, when I have little else to do, I read my second book, Dorothy L. Sayers's translation of Dante's *Inferno*. At first I felt self-conscious about reading such a book in such a place. But now, four days after arriving at Auschwitz, after four days of seeing gas chambers and ponds filled with ashes, after four days of mass gallows and starvation cells, I'm relieved to return to my room and read about how those who tried to predict the future would have their heads twisted 180 degrees. Such comically impossible, such metaphorically appropriate punishment makes far more sense than a medical ward where inmates received injections that killed them instead of curing them and where they were led to a shower that murdered them.

* * *

There are three main camps in the Auschwitz complex. Auschwitz I, the original camp, was mostly a site where Polish political prisoners were kept. It was the site of the first gassings in the camp, which took place in the camp's mortuary, renovated for that purpose. However, most of the gassings took place in Auschwitz II, generally known as Birkenau. Those who were not immediately killed upon arrival worked in satellite labor camps, of which Auschwitz III, called Monowitz, was the largest.

Monowitz is my destination this gray morning, the reason I have walked the two miles into town. Last night I asked a taxi driver in the Auschwitz museum parking lot how much it might cost to go there, and when he gave me a price that was more than the nightly rate of my room at the Centrum, I decided I would walk.

Heading toward Monowitz, located on the other side of town, I think about what I've seen the last few days. At Auschwitz the same barracks that housed the Polish prisoners still stand. Now they contain exhibits on the camp's history as well as the evidence of the crimes committed there: mountains of shoes, suitcases, brushes, eyeglasses, and the shorn hair of women, not yet shipped to Germany to be made into haircloth when the Soviets arrived in January 1945. After its founding in 1947, the State Museum of Auschwitz-Birkenau restored the gas chamber, which had been converted into an air-raid shelter in 1943, after the much larger crematoriums of Birkenau went into operation. The museum staff reinstalled the original ovens and rebuilt the chimney, and now it is possible, after walking past a black stone marker, to stand in the spot where thousands of people died, to close one's eyes and imagine, in vain, what it might have been like to die there. Auschwitz is now evidence, the extant site. Walking there alongside the barbed wire and guard towers, I sometimes feel as though the Germans have just left.

Birkenau, on the other hand, is a ruin. With the Soviets approaching from the east, the Germans ceased killing operations in November 1944 and began dismantling the crematoriums, attempting to cover up the evidence of their crimes. In January 1945, just days before the Red Army arrived, they blew up the three remaining buildings (Krema IV having been destroyed in an attempted uprising by Jewish workers a few months earlier). Of the three hundred or so barracks that housed hundreds of thousands of prisoners, about fifty remain, the rest reduced to the brick chimneys that still occasionally crumble to the ground, reminders that this place was supposed to be only temporary.

Monowitz, which I'm slowly moving toward, is apparently just a monument, a simple installation on the former site of the prison camp. The Monowitz monument does a lot of work; it stands not only for that subcamp but also the twenty-seven other subcamps of Auschwitz, places where prisoners (including Primo Levi) labored for the German war cause. When in 1947 the Polish government set aside Auschwitz and Birkenau as historical sites worthy of commemoration, they neglected to do so for Monowitz; as a result, nothing remains of the camp but a monument marking where it once stood.

And then there is Oświęcim, the town unfortunate enough to be chosen by Heinrich Himmler, *Reichsführer* of the SS, as the center for the final solution of the "Jewish Question." Between evidence and ruin and monument, it sits, trapped by its own history, all these juxtapositions of time and place, tour buses arriving in the parking lots not for the night heron but for the place where night descended.

What am I doing here?

I'm asking this on a few levels. Frankl argues that a "will to meaning" drives humanity as much as any pleasure principle or survival instinct, that we try to give our lives some sort of meaning, "something by which to live." I suppose that I'm trying to find some sort of meaning here at Auschwitz.

I became aware of the Holocaust, and by extension, Auschwitz, in fifth grade. In our social studies class we covered the basics: Hitler, six million Jews, the yellow stars of David, Anne Frank, the gas chambers. I read a book, a Choose Your Own Adventure–type in a series called "Time Machine," in which the reader had to go back to the Warsaw Ghetto in order to uncover the location of a cache of documents. A series of choices led me to Auschwitz, where I observed inmates headed toward the gas chambers before I "jumped" in time back to Warsaw.

The unit couldn't have lasted long, but despite that, I kept thinking about Auschwitz, trying to picture it in my mind, trying to see the gas chambers disguised as showers, trying to see the trains arriving. *How could that have happened?* I wondered, and then, *I should go there and see it.*

For me as for so many others, Auschwitz became the Holocaust itself. This was how it happened: they were rounded up, they came on trains, they were killed in gas chambers at Auschwitz.

Now I am here, eighteen years later. I have seen all the things I have read about: the metal gate reading *"ARBEIT MACHT FREI"* under which the prisoners marched each day on their way to work, the steps that lead down to the ruins of the disrobing room of the gas chambers, the guard tower at Birkenau that seems to be pictured in every history book, the piles of hair and shoes and pots and empty cans that once held Zyklon B pellets.

Yet I'm not sure that I understand this place any better after having been here for a few days. Even though the sight of the metal gate of Auschwitz and the guard tower of Birkenau were enough to stop me, literally, in my tracks—*they're real, they really exist*—I still don't know how to talk, much less write, about what I've seen.

So I've decided that the way to do that, the path to understanding, is to see *everything,* to be the anti-tourist, to be a traveler, to have a stake in what I'm seeing, to map out and track down every last monument and memorial, to understand the scope and enormity of the site. "Down we must go, to that dark world and blind," Virgil tells Dante at the entrance to Hell. "According to logotherapy," writes Frankl, "we can discover this meaning in life in three different ways: (1) by doing a deed; (2) by experiencing a value; and (3) by suffering."

If I do this, I tell myself, *surely I will know the place, the evidence, the ruins, the monuments. All of it. And then maybe I'll know what I'm doing here.*

* * *

I ran out of film yesterday while taking pictures at Birkenau of the water cisterns near Kremas II and III, so while walking to the Monowitz monument, I keep an eye out for camera stores. After a half hour of walking, I begin to realize that nothing's going to be open today—all the supermarkets I check are closed, and the one gas station that I find doesn't carry any film.

Even though I know that Oświęcim functions as a town now, it still seems impossible that I should be able to do things as mundane as buy groceries or gas here. I feel as though the town should have frozen in the late 1940s and, like the camps, been set aside, declared unusable because of the significance of what happened there.

When my train arrived a few days ago, I bought groceries at a small store that I found in a residential neighborhood on the other side of the State Museum. I shopped as though I was twelve years old, filling up my basket with Nutella, bread, sodas, and an onion-flavored corn chip called "Mr. Snaki." I bought bottles of raspberry-flavored beer and Okocim dark lager and walked back to the hotel, a plastic bag in each hand to eat a meal that my parents would never consider dinner.

I walked past a playground where children ran around while their parents watched, passed young couples out for a stroll in the early evening. The sun was low, the light hitting the Communist-era high-rise apartments and making the painted concrete shine with a loveliness they should not have possessed.

It was a beautiful June evening, the very beginning of summer, and as I walked back, I looked at brick houses, wondering if they were built from the bricks of the *krema* or of the barracks. I walked through a park with a sunken center and a plaque declaring it to be the site of a mass grave, filled with the bodies of hundreds of prisoners who died after liberation. And I passed Auschwitz itself, the gas chamber chimney glowing red in the sunset.

Auschwitz bleeds into Oświęcim. The town is forever its former self, a colossal graveyard, a monstrous evidence file, a monumental monument.

* * *

At an intersection, just past a quietly busy Sunday flea market, I come upon Oświęcim's Jewish cemetery, closed this early in the morning. As I cross over to it, I'm surprised that it's still here, still maintained, given the extermination of the town's Jewish populace, as well as the destruction of Jewish cemeteries in other towns in Poland.

I peer through the gate at tombstones set in rows, similar to the Jewish cemeteries in Warsaw and Kraków. At those places, however, there were attendants and guides. In Kraków I worked my way around tour groups leaving written prayers at the graves of *tzaddiks*, or wise men. I look around the cemetery, trying to see if any folded pieces of paper lay scattered around any particular grave, but I can't find them.

The Jewish cemeteries in Warsaw and Kraków felt like part of the community, however reduced by the Holocaust those communities might have been. In Oświęcim, though, the Jewish cemetery feels like a monument that existed before the event it commemorates, a graveyard that must be reevaluated and reassigned meaning in the wake of what happened after it. It feels like yet another reminder of the necropolis, the city of the dead, that encroaches upon Oświęcim at all times, the triple fence of barbed wire that surrounds Auschwitz but keeps the city contained as well.

* * *

After the establishment of the State Museum, each country was invited to establish an exhibition in one of the former barracks of Auschwitz. They still exist, although all the exhibitions have changed over time, through Communist and post-Communist governments. The vast majority of them now tell similar stories, which I realize after walking through a half dozen of them: *we suffered; our Jews suffered; yes, it's true, some of us collaborated, but many of us resisted, too.*

Many of the exhibitions seem to reflect the general character of their countries. The Netherlands exhibit is clean, well-lit, and particularly informative. Italy's, in contrast, is nothing but a vortex of fabric, stretching through several rooms, that offers wordless comment. France's, rededicated in January 2005 during the ceremonies commemorating the sixtieth anniversary of the camp's liberation, is well-designed, though a little standoffish. The USSR's is closed for renovations.

Poland's exhibit is defensive. Often it leaves Auschwitz entirely in order to bring up Poland's suffering during the war in general; it mentions the nonaggression pact between Germany and the USSR that divided the country between two sets of invaders in 1939, as well as the Katyn massacre of Polish soldiers and citizens by Soviet troops during the war, the existence of which was never fully admitted until after Poland elected a democratic government.

All this reminds me of the fact that Auschwitz, especially during the first twenty years of its existence as a memorial site, was essentially a site of Polish commemoration and martyrdom. Poland thought of itself as "Christ among the nations," a sacrificial lamb of Europe, and for a long time, Poles, not Jews, were the focus of the site. Tellingly, Birkenau was left mostly unvisited (and, to an extent, unprotected) for many years, and although the fact that Jews made up the vast majority of victims at Auschwitz was never denied, the exhibitions downplayed that fact, preferring instead to present the camp as a memorial to the victims of fascism—socialism's greatest enemy.

In 1967 dignitaries finally unveiled a long awaited memorial at Birkenau, installed partially in response to mounting pressures from outside Poland, including a large number of Jewish visitors coming to see the sites of their families' destruction. And in 1968 the State Museum opened an exhibit called "The Martyrology and Struggle of the Jews" in Barracks #27, where the carved inscription in a stone in the final room asked, "Cain, what have you done with your brother Abel?"

The stone is gone now—the exhibit was remodeled in 1978—but the current Jewish exhibition, like the other national exhibitions, is rarely visited by tourists. Emerging from each one, I see tour groups walking past on their way from the execution block to the reconstructed mass gallows. I suppose their tour guide gives them the history; they don't need it presented over and over again from each country's point of view.

Auschwitz lets itself stand as a monument. Apart from the black stone marker at the entrance to the rebuilt gas chamber and a redesigned cell door, incorporating a stylized lamp, at the site of Polish martyr Maximilian Kölbe's death, there is nothing that resembles a traditional monument—no obelisk, no commemorative plaque. Flowers pile up at the base of the black wall in the execution block, and candles are lit within the gas chamber, but nothing at Auschwitz has a monument that negotiates its traumatic history. Sometimes all you need to see in order to understand that people died in a gas chamber is a gas chamber.

Gazing up into the sky, I wonder if the raindrop that just hit my arm is the first of many or only a suggestion of what may come in the next few hours. Nothing else follows it, so I keep walking. I would have kept walking anyway.

At this point I have crossed through most of Oświęcim, into its industrial sector. Instead of passing by storefronts and restaurants (closed, of course), I'm now walking by factories and warehouses. The steel structures tower over the town, smokestacks filling the sky with white smoke. I wonder if any of these are from the synthetic rubber plant that drove the camp's expansion. The I. G. Farben company chose to build a plant in Auschwitz because of the camp's supply of slave labor and the town's location on the rail system. In turn, the camp grew larger to meet the demand from the factory, which led, in part, to Himmler's decision to centralize the killing process at the Birkenau camp.

Unlike at Auschwitz and Birkenau, I don't really know what I'm looking for here. I've never seen a picture of the monument at Monowitz and only know of its existence because I asked an attendant at Auschwitz a few days earlier. I assume I'll know it when I see it.

* * *

Among the ruins of Birkenau there are a few more memorials, though not many: an obelisk for the Sinti and Roma, hidden behind the barbed wire of their assigned section of the camp; a small white marker for French nationals who died in the camp, located in the women's camp; a larger, concrete memorial at the site of the mass grave of Soviet POWs, the first victims of the gas chambers in 1941, far beyond the camp's perimeter; and more of the black stone markers, at the sites where ashes were dumped into ponds or buried in fields, or at the locations at the edges of the camp where the first temporary gas chambers stood.

And then there is the Monument to the Victims of Fascism, the 1967 monument. It stands between Kremas II and III, at the opposite end of the camp from the famous watchtower. One day I find a group of Israeli soldiers placing a wreath not at the monument, but near it, at the end of the railroad tracks that run alongside the selection ramp. As they go through the ceremony—including music and speeches and military precision in their actions—the monument stands behind them like the afterthought it essentially was.

Birkenau, unlike Auschwitz, has a number of monuments, but, like those at Auschwitz, they feel superfluous, unnecessary. At the edge of one of the ponds, I kneel down and pick at the ground, having heard a tour guide tell her group that all the white flecks around the pond are ashes, still there after sixty years. Looking at a piece of ash not much bigger than a grain of rice, I realize, horrified, that this bit of ash is actually a chip of bone, the bone of someone murdered sixty years ago in a crematorium not twenty feet from me, whose body was then burned in an oven and the ashes dumped into a stagnant pond.

With Birkenau itself refusing to hide its dead, with the bones of the murdered surfacing at the end of the tracks, what use is an abstract monument for those soldiers?

* * *

Looking down the road, I can see an intersection of some sort and a gas station, and I realize that I must be approaching the Monowitz site, if only for the reason that I'm shrinking the territory it could possibly be in. I press on and continue down the sidewalk, passing only a woman pushing a stroller while cars zoom along the road. I spot a green space, start angling toward it, and see something promising—a clearing by the highway, with some sort of structure on it.

I'm still crossing the street when I make out the details and understand that this must be the Monowitz monument. It's not a large monument, especially when compared to the sprawling Birkenau monument, but it's effective enough: rough concrete stacked to resemble the fence posts of the Auschwitz complex, with sharp angles of metal that call to mind barbed wire crossing them in three places. At the base of the posts, a tangle of tortured metal figures rests. A nearby plaque explains that this was the site of the Monowitz subcamp.

Beyond the official monument, other monuments stand: the factories of companies, many of which used and profited from Monowitz's slave labor, which helped the camp toward its eventual size, which supplied Auschwitz with Zyklon B for the gas chambers, whose cremation experts traveled to the camp to witness executions and suggested methods to improve them. Many are in business still, although some have gone to certain lengths to acknowledge their guilt.

Dozens, hundreds even, of companies and corporations that, despite their regret or lack thereof, are still inextricably intertwined with Auschwitz. They work in Oświęcim, but they cannot avoid the ghosts of those who, unwillingly, ran their machines and toiled in their workshops. Everything pushes to the top: the bricks, the memorials, the chips of bone that appear after each rain, even sixty years later. Nothing can be kept hidden.

* * *

Catholics go to confession, one of the bits of doctrine that differentiates us from Protestants. When I am cognizant of my sinfulness, I am supposed to make a confession to a priest, who will absolve me of my sin.

So here goes: I am a thief. When I first held the bit of bone in my hand, I did not return it to the mud of the pond where it had been dumped six decades earlier; instead, I put it in my shirt pocket and walked away. I have stolen part of a murdered person's body—man or woman, child or adult, I do not know—all because I was attempting to understand what had happened at a certain place at a certain time, because I could not make meaning out of the monuments there. I stole to try to understand.

I walked around Birkenau with the bone in my pocket. I thought of saints' relics, bits of bone and cloth enshrined in the altars of Catholic churches. I thought of the Israelis I'd seen, young Jews who'd come to their site of martyrdom, at the end of the railroad spur marking the end of the world. I thought of the eighth circle of Dante's Hell, where the thieves are placed, of how they lose their identities and forms there, the distinction between themselves and others gone in the afterlife because they could not make that distinction while alive.

* * *

I am not a Jew. I'm a tourist, not a traveler. The people I can understand here are not the Israeli soldiers laying a wreath at the tracks' end. My people here are the Polish citizens, the bystanders, not the victims, the ones who saw their town transformed into the final destination and forever marked as the end of the world, frozen like the bottom of Dante's inferno.

A few hours later, I walked back to the ash pond and pressed the chip of bone back into the earth, muddying my hand as I did so.

FOUR: GO NOW IN PEACE

Two days after my walk across the town, I stand on the platform at the Oświęcim train station, waiting for the train to take me back to Kraków. I've eaten a final meal at the Centrum and thanked the staff as best as I could for their hospitality. I feel like I've seen everything I could see here, although I'm just as sure that I've missed something. I know this site as well as any bystander, anyone not directly connected with it, could.

I don't understand the language, but I know what has happened here.

I am, like the city, now inextricably linked with Auschwitz. And when, as he or she will doubtlessly in the next ten years, the last remaining firsthand witness of what took place here, bystander, victim, or perpetrator, dies, the task will fall to everything else—evidence, ruins, monuments, cities, historians, and even visitors like me—to recreate Auschwitz, to keep the fact of it rising to the surface, to keep it from disappearing into Oświęcim and the void of forgotten history.

The train arrives, idling on the track for a few minutes to let the few Kraków-bound travelers this morning board. I find an empty car and sit down on the cracked vinyl seat, open my copy of Dante to the final canto, where he emerges, "back to the lit world." And before long, the train sets off, and Oświęcim slips away quickly.

Perpetrators

UNDRAWN LINES

I remember the Nazi Boys of junior high, the ones who doodled swastikas endlessly in the margins of their notebooks, who looked up *Mein Kampf* in the card catalog of the school library, who wore all black and faux Iron Crosses they'd found at swap meets and auto shows. They lingered over the photos of corpses in the history books, did reports on Hitler and his lieutenants in social studies class. They were scary, grew long, yellow fingernails; they had facial hair before anyone else. It wasn't difficult to imagine them cruel in another time, another place. They were outside of the social circles. I was too, so I noticed them.

I remember myself in junior high as well, a reed of a boy-child, moved by stories of hiding and survival, things I wanted from those days of bullies and lockers. I studied the Holocaust too, thought often, too often, about the showers and ovens.

The Nazi Boys: I knew them, got along OK with them. But I want to say that I didn't get the allure of the marching and the murder the way they did.

I hope I didn't. I hope I ended up different from them, hope that when I went to Poland and Germany I went because I wanted to sympathize and understand, not to rubberneck at a murder scene.

* * *

This is what the monument looks like: a field of rectangular stones called *stelae,* 2,711 of them, all black, filling a massive city block. They are about seven feet long, about three feet wide, and range in height from flush with the ground to over twelve feet high, about twice my height. The space between each one is even, wide enough for a wheelchair to pass through, but not enough for two people to walk side by side. Each person must pass through the monument alone. There is no specific route through the stelae, which, despite the architect's insistence that they do not represent anything in particular, look distinctly like a field of black sarcophagi.

Each of the stelae sits upon its own foundation, which means that each one tilts in its own direction, though none does so dramatically. The monument is always open, although the information center beneath it only admits visitors between 10 and 8 each day. On a rainy day, such as the day I visited the monument, the stelae glisten with water, and visitors can imagine that they see themselves reflected in them.

* * *

As I arrived in Berlin, less than a month after Germany had dedicated the Memorial to the Murdered Jews of Europe, its long-delayed Holocaust memorial, I was happy. Ecstatic, even. I practically bounded off the train and danced my way through Zoo Station (*Zoo Station!* I thought. *I've heard of this place!*).

I had been in Poland for the previous two weeks, a grim tour of extermination camps and massacre sites, of the ruined shells of bombed-out buildings and the remnants of gas chambers. Auschwitz. Treblinka. I found one of the last remaining lengths of the Warsaw Ghetto wall in the courtyard of an apartment building, ran my hands over its rough brick. I dug bone fragments out of the mud and held them in my hand. I wept in front of a display case filled with shoes.

And now I was out. I was free. I'd left the nightmare of twentieth-century Europe for the capital of twenty-first-century Europe. Sure, there was some work to do with history here, but there was also modern architecture and Haribo gummi bears and, at the end, a train ride to Frankfurt and an airplane pointed toward home.

I was thrilled.

Before I'd left for Poland, I'd asked a friend who'd lived there for a few years if I needed to learn much Polish.

"Not really," he said. "Practically everyone under forty speaks English."

"Great," I said, and memorized *czecz* (hello), *dziekuje* (thank you), and *czy mowi pani po angielsku?* (do you speak English?).

Upon arriving in Poland, I was looking for a memorial in the city of Poznan. I couldn't find it, so I found someone about thirty years old in a square.

"*Chee movie pan po angleyesku?*" I asked in my best phonetic Polish.

He shook his head slowly. "*Nie,*" he said.

Nie, everyone said. I spent two weeks out of conversation with anyone; then I arrived in Berlin.

In Berlin I realized that I wasn't sure how to get to my hostel, so I stopped in the railway station office, nervous, since I spoke as much German as I did Polish.

Me, to the station agent: "*Sprechen sie English?*"

The station agent: "I speak a little bit of English, although my knowledge is not as strong as it could be. I will try to help you, though."

Again: joy at arriving in Berlin.

* * *

Berlin's Holocaust Memorial—officially dedicated on the twelfth of May 2005, sixty years and four days after the German surrender and a month before I arrived—serves an unusual purpose for a monument. Although it commemorates the dead, as many monuments do, it does not stand at the site of their death. The Berlin memorial is far removed from Auschwitz or Treblinka, even from the Sachsenhausen concentration camp on the outskirts of town, from the forests of the Eastern front where the *Einsatzgruppen* mobile killing squads executed one million Jews, from the ghettos of Poland or Czechoslovakia or any of the other fifteen countries from which Jewish men and women were selected to die.

It is a memorial not on the site of action, but on the site of decision; not the site of the gun put to the head, but the pen put to paper; not the site of gas filling a room, but of men sitting in conference. It is a memorial to the victims of a crime, but unlike almost every other monument on earth, it was built by the perpetrators of that crime. Berlin's memorial is not a monument of grief; it is a monument of guilt, the confession of Germany, placed in the center of the rebuilt city.

* * *

The rain comes at intervals this early June day while I wait in line behind a school group to enter the Reichstag, the building that houses Germany's governing body. Each time the rain starts back up, I lift the hood of my jacket over my head and lean forward, trying to get myself under the umbrella of the teacher in front of me.

The reunified Germans take a particular pride in the Reichstag; it was burned by an arsonist's torch almost immediately after Adolf Hitler became chancellor in 1933, which meant that the Nazis never ruled from it—something the exhibit inside the building points out with pride. When Germany reunified and Berlin became its capital once again, the building was renovated, and the architect Sir Norman Foster built a glass dome on top to replace the one destroyed in World War II.

It's this dome that I'm waiting to get up to, and although the rain is starting to soak through my jacket, I'm grateful for it, because it keeps the line short. Each group enters, about fifty people at a time, passes through security, and then gathers onto an elevator that takes them up to the building's roof, where they can walk up a spiral ramp to the top of Foster's dome and look down into the legislative chamber—an architectural metaphor for the transparency of government and a reminder of the people's responsibility to monitor their representatives. After all, the front of the Reichstag proclaims in Gothic lettering *Dem Deutscher Volke*—For the German People.

After entering the building and walking up the ramp, I zip up my jacket. The dome is open to the elements, and the wind blows strong enough to make the huge German flags snap violently.

At the dome's summit, I look over the city in all directions. I look far out, toward the edges of the city, to the TV tower in the former East Berlin and the Spree River, snaking its way through the center. I see the glass circus tent of Sony's European headquarters, built in the former "death zone" of the wall, now the revitalized Potsdamer Platz. I see the Brandenberg Gate and, a block away, the field of stelae, glowing with the lights set along the paths between them.

I am a tourist here, just thirty-six hours in the city before I return home, a day and a half to see what I want to see. I can see all of Berlin from up here, 360 degrees of the ruined and rebuilt capital, but I cannot see what I know to be out there. I want to find the Berliners among me, grab them by the arm and pull them to the railing, telling them, *Point it out to me. Show me where it ended. Show me where Hitler died by his own hand, where his aides burned his body. I can see where you remember, but not where you're trying to forget.*

* * *

The trouble with a monument is that it finalizes memory, that it literally makes concrete what we remember, and we are fated—cursed?—to remember that event or person through its conduit of memory. The monument makes history the past; it ends the event, announces its completion. There is the danger of satisfaction with the story the monument tells.

So far the Memorial to the Murdered Jews of Europe has not allowed Germany to move on. Its design and construction, always contentious, provided the country with a forum in which to debate its guilt and its seemingly unending penance for the twentieth century's greatest crime. A group of citizens, calling themselves the Initiative against Drawing a Final Line with the Past, called for open and renewed discussion of not only the Holocaust but of German anti-Semitism in general. Their actions suggest an awareness of the monument's potential to draw *ein Schlußstrich*—that final line—in the drawing of the stark lines of Berlin's Holocaust Memorial.

At first the memorial was to be a three-hundred-foot square of concrete, engraved with the names of as many victims of the Nazi years as possible, and room reserved for the unknown names. Such a proposal echoes facilities like Yad Vashem's Hall of Names and its library of biographical data, only carved in stone—made a monument, and, presumably, more permanent.

A monument, however, doesn't have to contain historical information. It doesn't have to be a library, or a repository. What it does is represent history and memory in a collective, aesthetic way. Many of the most iconic monuments and memorials—the Washington Monument, the Arc de Triomphe, the Taj Mahal, to name just a few—operate independent of their text, their historical information.

The problem with the early version of the Memorial to the Murdered Jews of Europe is that reserving a place for each victim's name assumes that the list can be completed at some point in the future. It assumes that the Holocaust can be known, understood fully.

The field of stelae operate differently. Architect Peter Eisenman's design, absent of any interpretive text, admits the fundamental incomprehension of the Holocaust. The number of stelae—2,711—refers to nothing. The monument doesn't attempt to delineate who was and was not a victim of the Nazi years, as any project involving individual names might. It memorializes them conceptually, those who died anonymously in a thousand different places. The monument marks the tragedy of those who cannot be known, those made invisible by the Third Reich's bureaucrats in offices not far from its site.

But another kind of place, a historical site that remains unmarked, whether by neglect or conscious decision, carries with it the risk of remaining undefined. This place, an "unmonument," leaves the story of history unfinished, makes the end of the sentence a question mark rather than a period. In the study of history, a field where the desire for specificity reigns, an unmonument is an uncomfortable unknown. It is the trail dying out at the detective's feet.

I've often wondered if historical sites carry with them an innate psychic residue, as though the events that happened there left some sort of invisible trace. Could I tell, dropped into any field, if a battle had raged there a century earlier? Would I simply *know* that a murder had happened in a room?

That evening in Berlin, the stelae glowing, I scanned the neighborhood for signs of *der Führerbunker,* for the site to speak to me. I haunted the streets of Berlin, listening for ghosts. I boarded a U-Bahn train traveling in the wrong direction, circled the city, from the center out to the west and then to the east. And I heard nothing.

* * *

The next morning, I took the train back into the center of the city to see a place that at one time had been considered for the memorial, a place with more than traces of history and atrocity.

In May 1933 the newly ascendant Nazi Party chose an art school building at Prinz-Albrecht-Strasse 8 as the location for the *Geheime Staatspolizei,* or Gestapo. Not long after, the SS moved its operations next door, followed shortly by the SD, the Security Service of the SS. In 1939 the Gestapo, the criminal police, and the SD were united into a single agency; Prinz-Albrecht-Strasse 8 was its official headquarters.

For a dozen years, in various ways, the building at this address was the nexus of planning death. Then, like much of wartime Berlin, the building was destroyed, leaving only its lower levels—the cells in which prisoners were held, tortured, and executed.

I'm looking at these cells now. They're rough, crumbling half rooms, exposed to the elements. I think of Freud and the subconscious, how the basement is the hidden room, where we hide what we don't want shown. And here is an evil place laid out in the open for all to see.

And yet it's not quite right. Building the Holocaust Memorial here would overrun the dozens of other layers of history here, ignoring political prisoners and Communists, socialists and homosexuals and plain criminals who were trapped in this corner of hell.

To add to the problematic nature of the site: one of the last intact sections of the Berlin Wall runs along the top of the excavation. History piles up; sorting through it here would be like drilling a core sample and trying to analyze its strata. We would ignore too much.

* * *

I am of the third generation of the Cold War. My parents were part of the first generation: my mother born the year Julius and Ethel Rosenberg were arrested as Soviet spies. She remembers watching the film *Duck and Cover* in grade school, learning to mimic the turtle who hides in his shell when he sees the flash of the atomic bomb. They were children of Truman and Eisenhower, their memorial marked 1945–1961, their Berlin divided into four sectors overseen by the Allies.

My father's younger brothers, my uncles, are of the middle generation of the Cold War. They knew SALT and Vietnam, wars fought by proxy rather than atomic weapons. They are 1962 to 1975, beginning with the Cuban Missile Crisis and ending with the evacuation from the US Embassy in Saigon. They grew up with a Berlin that had grown a wall through its heart.

And I, the third generation, grew up with the stories of the first and second. I knew Reagan, was terrified of him and his press conference joking: *I have just signed legislation outlawing Russia forever. The bombing begins in five minutes.* I was convinced of "mutually assured destruction," of a slow death for the survivors, of a Berlin forever divided. I learned of the "death zone" of the wall, that no-man's-land where the East German soldiers shot those who tried to escape. I learned two capitals for a single country.

The Cold War was a forty-four-year slow burn across the consciousness of our lives. I fervently believed that it would end in fire, that the tanks and missiles would race across Europe, that Berlin was the place where the Cold War would go hot.

And then I came home from school to see Germans on television swinging sledgehammers and reaching through the holes in the no-longer-permanent wall. The news then was already full of the revolutions happening in the mysterious East—Poland transitioning away from Communism, Hungary opening its border—but this, the wall going to pieces. Suddenly it was all very real to me.

I was thirteen years old when the wall fell—the age at which a Jewish boy becomes a man, the age at which a Catholic boy in Kansas is confirmed into the faith, making an adult's decision to join the Holy Roman Church. I chose "Vincent" as my confirmation name to honor my recently deceased grandfather, but rather than the better-known Vincent de Paul, I chose Saint Vincent Ferrer as my patron. My grandfather had been a man who worked with his hands, and Vincent Ferrer was the patron of builders, construction workers, plumbers.

At thirteen, watching the footage from Berlin's solid line turning dotted, I was no builder. My hands were soft, pink, virgin. Watching the footage, they ached to hold a hammer, to swing a pickax.

* * *

My childhood fear of nuclear destruction vanished under the sledgehammers of the "wallpeckers," and I took my first steps into manhood as a society lost the faith it had known for forty-four years.

So you might understand, then, how I felt upon arriving in Berlin. The city had never been the Holocaust for me the way that the ideas of Auschwitz or Treblinka or even Germany as a whole had. The people around me looked like me, like my mother's side of the family, a few centuries removed from the Black Forest.

There, at a remaining scrap of the nightmare wall of my childhood that had pockmarked and broken by thousands, I turned away from the laid-out lines of history. I wanted to find the last thing I wanted to see. I wanted to escape history, to put behind these ghosts.

I knew where to go; I turned away from the wall, from Prinz-Albrecht-Strasse 8, and headed north along Wilhelmstrasse. The unmarked and unknown lay ahead.

* * *

At the end this is what the unmonument looks like: a few apartment buildings, several stories high, nondescript. Since the wall ran close to here, the apartments were reserved for low-threat citizens, who were unlikely to defect: government officials and their families, mostly, although sometimes also the Olympic athletes. At the entrance to one of the apartment buildings, there is a garden, a few children's toys scattered around it. There is no marker, no sign, no stone statue or bronze plaque to inform passersby of the significance of this site, of the time sixty years ago when a man destroyed himself after destroying his country, after almost destroying a people.

Each apartment building sits impassively, standing a quiet, strange guard over the monument, the field of black stelae a block away that is Berlin's new Memorial to the Murdered Jews of Europe. And on a rainy day, such as the day I visited the monument, dozens of tourists and visitors will hurry past the unmonument at the apartment building's garden, past the slight depression in the grass, unaware that their wet footsteps push on the ground that buries the sealed, unmarked *Führerbunker.*

* * *

I found it, the unmonument, the *Führerbunker.* It's barely a stone's throw from the memorial. You'd walk by it, too, and never notice what you were walking by.

I found it and stood there on top of an obscured history. The day was overcast. I looked at nothing, really. The trappings of urban apartment life. I thought, *That's it. This is all there is.*

I thought, *Maybe it's best to leave some history unmarked.*

I thought, *Maybe drawing a line underneath something doesn't mean we forget that thing.*

And I thought, *Maybe if the monument and the unmonument can meet, if my Berlin joy can exist with this sorrow, then maybe we can continue being human.*

* * *

The unmonument works to keep itself unknown, to hide the past away. But if we were to mark it, would *der Führerbunker* be the site to commemorate? Even Hitler's death was not Hitler's end. Would we put the marker in the city of Rathenow, in eastern Germany, where his charred body was buried by the KGB and where it remained for twenty-five years? Would there be a sign by the Elbe River where in 1970 his ashes were dumped, finally cremated after the failed attempt by his staff as Berlin itself burned?

Or would we guide visitors to the room in Moscow where the pieces of his skull, bullet-broken, reside in a box, or the other room, elsewhere in the city, where his teeth, the means by which he was identified after death, lay in another cardboard box?

Hitler finally retreated to Berlin in November 1944, having spent most of the war in his *Wolfßchanze,* the Wolf's Lair, in northeastern Poland. *Der Führerbunker* was only a waiting room for a graveyard, an open grave waiting to be filled in with his body.

The unmonument does not draw the final line. The unmonument does not end the story of history. The unmonument merely waits to be uncovered, to be another piece of an infinite puzzle. It does not glow like the stelae at night.

* * *

Perhaps that explains the official name. It is not the "Berlin Holocaust Memorial" but the "Memorial to the Murdered Jews of Europe," terrifying in its specificity of crime and victim. The stelae may be abstract visually, but their intent is never doubted. This is not a memorial for all Germans who suffered in the Second World War, not a memorial for all victims of Nazism. It does not remember the Communists and homosexuals and Roma and Sinti and Jehovah's Witnesses and the others who died in the camps because of who they were.

It is the Jews' memorial, 2,711 reminders of what ordinary Germans did to ordinary Jews, their sins of commission and omission in the heart of their reunified capital.

* * *

And me? I felt the long train of history slowing for me. I had traveled through historian Raul Hilberg's trio of Holocaust participants: the victims in the seventeen thousand stones of the Treblinka death camp site, the bystanders in the small Polish town next to the mammoth Auschwitz complex, and now here, standing at the place where the perpetrators' *führer* finished himself, where the Thousand-Year Reich ended 988 years ahead of schedule with a bang and a whimper.

I knew that I couldn't ever escape history completely, no matter what I might have wished. The next year, Berlin would put up an explanatory sign at the apartment complex: a question answered. Four years later DNA testing would reveal that the skull fragments in Moscow actually belonged to a woman between twenty and forty years of age, an answer that was questioned.

* * *

It will always be a cloth, forever unraveling while it is woven, forever in flux, no matter how desperately we try to fix it with our stone and steel. But there, at a still-empty site, I felt done, a strange kind of happy. It was enough.

I thought about going back to the Memorial to the Murdered Jews of Europe. I wanted to see it again as a souvenir, as an object that helps us remember; I wanted to see it last, make it my last moment in Berlin. From the apartment complex, I took a few steps toward it. Then I turned.

I walked the other direction, back toward the U-Bahn station to catch a train that would take me back to the hostel to retrieve my backpack, and then to the train that would take me from Berlin, from its monument and its unmonument, from its memory and its forgetting.

A for Ache

I read once that an infant's brain at birth is completely smooth, and only as the child begins to process information coming from outside does the brain form the kinks and bends that give it its familiar shape. The events of our lives, no matter how minute, leave a physical reminder upon our brains, a scar painlessly made. Is a headache, then, the result of our experiences rubbing against each other too much? The pounding of our temples not the product of stress or restricted blood flow, but of our memories crashing into each other?

Once formed, a scar is relatively painless in comparison with the rest of our bodies. Like the monument, it is the dead part of the living world. But if amputees can still feel phantom pains in missing arms and legs, then we must also be able to feel the lack of our bodies, the places where part of us has been removed, cut, punctured, violated, invaded.

When I was eleven years old, I was sick and didn't know why. One morning I had swung my legs over the bed, and when the right one hit the ground, I screamed. Something hurt, deep in the bone.

There were a lot of tests: blood work, CAT scans, nuclear medicine. I grew to hate needles. Eventually the doctors decided to do a bone biopsy to see what they could find and scheduled the surgery for two days before Christmas. I was disappointed that I wouldn't be able to run down the stairs to see what Santa had brought, even though I'd learned the truth about him a few years earlier.

When I woke up in the recovery room, a nurse put my underwear on me (and such shame, at eleven years old, at my nudity, at the visibility of all my old scars), over the brace that now enclosed my right leg. But on Christmas Eve the doctors called my parents and told them that it wasn't cancer after all. They were excited; I didn't know why.

What I found out years later: the surgeon came out of the OR, told my parents that it was definitely cancer, that I had to lose the leg, and which one of them wanted to break the news to me? My mother demanded a second opinion, thus stopping further surgery, which is why I don't feel phantom pains from a missing limb.

In the decades since then, the bone removed in the biopsy has grown back, but the scar on my shin, at two and a half inches the most significant scar on my body, still gets noticed by people when I wear shorts. This is the scar that I tell a story about when the time comes to tell stories about our bodies with a new girlfriend, the postcoital moments when, oddly aware of our own nakedness, we try to explain ourselves, how we have come to look the way that we do. Because now, as we move from our twenties to our thirties, those of us who are still unmarried have collected enough scars, on our bodies and inside them, experience marking both our brains and our hearts, that we could tell each other epics.

And perhaps that's what's missing from me and the women at this point: a chance to see the end of the individual stories, the possibility of narrative lines converging. So many of us in this world, aching all over with regret and desire, our pasts the phantom pains we can never lose, only forget to remember.

The Definite Article

AT THE CLUB CALLED DÉJÀ VU

First song: she comes out, precarious on high platforms. She wears a black ensemble, as though in mourning. Her negligee flows out behind her, caught in the light diffracting off all the smoke in the room. She grasps the pole and swings herself around casually, testing her footing on high platform heels. Reassured, she shrugs the sheer negligee off, pushes it with her shoe toward the back of the stage. She looks out at the men sitting at the edge, all eyes on her. Their hands reach for dollar bills to lay in front of her.

She reaches a thin arm behind her back and grasps the string that holds her top on. She begins to pull. All the men stare at her, waiting. We all stare at her, waiting. I stare at her, waiting.

AT THE CEMETERY

I start that summer by visiting the tomb of Abraham Lincoln. The morning I do this is a bright clear morning, the sky a blue that looks like I could peel it off in long strips. The sun sits assuredly, with no clouds to distract from it.

I have always known of Lincoln, and Lincoln has always been mythology to me. As a child, I encountered an autograph of his and stared at it in devotion for hours. The stories I learned about him—the log cabin, the rail splitting, the walk through the snow to return the book—I believed in as fervently as I believed the story of Theseus and the Minotaur. My Lincoln seemed to ten-year-old me the perfect American, wise and fair, statesman and reluctant warrior, steadfast. Even revelations about his depression or the Marfan's syndrome couldn't dampen my enthusiasm for him.

Even after standing in front of it for a while, I'm still astonished by his tomb, at its size and its grandeur. I've become used to monuments that attempt to affect those who view them through their subtlety, quiet monuments that do not attempt to overwhelm but only try to create empathy. I'm too accustomed to a wall and a list of names. I understand a monument for the common people, not for great men.

Lincoln's tomb staggers me. I stand in the clear light of a May Illinois morning gazing up at the 117-foot-high obelisk, and I cannot even begin to comprehend the man. I feel like I have only now learned about him, and that I have heard only rumors for three decades, rumors that turn out to be true, one after the other, without a single falsehood in the bunch. I feel like the myth has turned out to be true, that the stick, thrown at my feet, has turned to a snake.

AT THE CLUB CALLED DÉJÀ VU

Her name—her stage name—is Honey. She is blonde and short, and when she undoes the knot that holds her top on, she does it as casually as if she were untying her shoe. She takes the bikini top over her head, still facing away from us, and for a moment all we see is her back, her shoulder blades and spine and the muscle and skin that cover them.

Before she turns to the men in the club, she wraps her arms around herself; then she spins around, eyes closed, and pauses for a moment. If the music were not so loud, and the air not so smoky, and the lights did not flash so much, she would look like she was asleep or about to make a wish. Perhaps she wishes she were not where she is.

Then she drops her arms.

INSIDE THE TOMB

No one speaks inside here. When I come around another bend and find people, I'm surprised that I can't hear them breathing in the silence. I feel as though I should apologize.

The tomb is ring-shaped. The eternity of Lincoln.

On the way around the ring, small sculptures and plaques describe Lincoln at various points in his life: young boy, Illinois lawyer, seated president.

In one alcove I find Daniel Chester French's sculpture. Lincoln's left hand is a loose fist: *A*. The index finger and thumb of his right hand point outward at a right angle: *L*. He signed into law the first college for the deaf. French remembered this, so his Lincoln speaks his name in American Sign Language. That's the story anyway.

The sculpture in the tomb is a small one; a larger version is depicted in miniature on the back of the bill I gave Honey last night as a tip. I feel like I should be worn out; I'm not even the least bit tired. I feel, or at least I want to feel, like a tireless pilgrim reaching the end of his journey, about to come into the presence of greatness, about to realize the enormity of his god. My Lincoln.

At the farthest point from the entrance, the top of the ring, where its jewel is set, I find the red marble marker, as big as an Egyptian sarcophagus. Under it is Lincoln. *The* Lincoln.

I still can't hear anyone breathe in this room.

AT THE CLUB CALLED DÉJÀ VU

Her breasts are small and white, and when the light hits them right, I can see blue veins running underneath the skin, a road map to her body. She makes her way around the stage, collecting tips after a short dance in front of each man. Her hands float over her breasts, brushing only slightly the nipples made erect by the club's overworked air conditioner. She drops to her knees and runs a finger over the fabric of her panties, hinting at what lies underneath.

The dollar bills flow to her. The men can't get them to her quickly enough. When she reaches the man next to me, she takes his dollar, folds it in half lengthwise, and places it between his teeth. Bending forward, she presses her breasts together and, leaning in to bury his face in them, takes his money between them. Then she turns to me.

How do I know that anything has happened? Only through monuments.

Dozens of them, statues and plaques and cannons, lie scattered across the lawn here in Kalamazoo, Michigan. The dead of so many wars are remembered in bronze and marble representations of themselves or in lists of names chiseled into polished black granite. Every town has this place, its square block of memory.

At my feet I find a small bronze marker, entirely invisible in the face of the rearing horse and steadfast soldier. I bend close to it and read the three magic words that begin so many of the monuments I have found: *On this site.*

In 1856, during John C. Frémont's presidential campaign, Lincoln delivered his only speech in Michigan in Kalamazoo, in support of the new Republican Party and its relationship to abolitionism: "Not to Democrats alone do I make this appeal, but to all who love these great and true principles. Come, and keep coming! Strike, and strike again! So sure as God lives, the victory shall be yours." And he did it right here, on the very patch of grass that I now stand on, more than 150 years later.

Which is, of course, impossible. The whole earth has shifted during those years. The grass Lincoln stood on is long dead, withered and frozen during seven score and seven winters. This park has been dug up a dozen times, landscaped and re-landscaped over and over again.

And all this assumes that the spot I'm standing in front of was the exact spot where Lincoln stood. How can I know? There's no one alive who saw Lincoln speak, maybe not even anyone alive whose grandparent might have heard him speak and could reliably point somewhere and say, "There. He stood there." History and its monuments depend on eyewitnesses and evidence, on unreliable narrators and uncertain memories.

So again I ask, How can I know anything? How can any monument be true? How can any statue or plaque pretend to permanence when everything, everything moves?

If the earth doesn't rest, where is Lincoln's body now? How many people pay their respects at an empty grave?

AT THE CLUB CALLED DÉJÀ VU

I've never been to an all-nude strip club before. The few strip clubs I have been to—fewer than one hand's worth of fingers—have been topless bars, where contact between dancers and patrons is illegal. Places where the dancers wear pasties that look like clear round Band-Aids, the kind my friends' mothers would have put on a small wound.

Here, though, I am shocked by what happens. Fantasy booths filled with men watching women simulate masturbating; a row of frames and mattresses, separated only by thin drapery, where the bed dances take place.

Honey turns to me, and when we make eye contact, she smiles and I look away, just barely, just for a second. She gyrates in front of me, turns around, bends over, and winks at me from between her legs.

She is acting, I know. *She is at work,* I tell myself.

When I hold out a dollar for her, she doesn't have me slide it between her hip and thong, the way they do at other clubs, nor does she place it between my teeth. Instead, she pulls open the front of her underwear, and when I try to tuck it in with minimal contact, she grabs my hand and shoves it down so that my fingers rub against the thin strip of pubic hair she has left.

Here, I feel like an embarrassed child.

FROM THE BROCHURE (SPRINGFIELD)

Lincoln returned to Springfield on a funeral train and was placed in the public receiving vault of the Oak Ridge Cemetery on May 4, 1865. His tomb was completed in 1874; he had been moved into it three years earlier.

It is open from 9 AM to 5 PM from March through October, 9 to 4 in the winter months. It is closed Presidents' Day, but not Lincoln's Birthday.

In the summer, the 114th Illinois Volunteer Reactivated Infantry holds a flag retreat ceremony. A selected visitor receives the flag each week.

Lincoln's remains are in a steel and concrete vault beneath the burial chamber.

AT THE CLUB CALLED DÉJÀ VU

And now we've reached the second song. Finished with the first round, Honey walks to the back of the stage, swings around the pole. Facing away from the men, she hooks her thumbs into the sides of her thong and inches the fabric downward, slowly revealing the cleft of her buttocks.

Once her underwear has crossed the fullest curve of her hips, she moves her hands away and the thong falls to the floor, all eyes following its path down her legs. She places her hands on her new-revealed skin, gently, as though touching herself for the first time. She doesn't need to turn her head to see that we are all reaching for the folded dollar bills in our pockets.

OUTSIDE THE CABIN, BUT INSIDE THE MONUMENT

Three miles south of Hodgenville, Kentucky, stands a neoclassical structure designed by John Russell Pope, who would later design the Jefferson Memorial in Washington, DC. This building looks like a prototype of that one, a little smaller with fewer columns and no dome. Inside this structure, up its fifty-six stairs and past the cornerstone laid by Theodore Roosevelt, is another building, architect unknown.

I have rounded the summer, Lincoln as the ring encompassing my summer travels; in May, as the days grew longer and hotter, I stood in Lincoln's tomb. Now on Labor Day, the end of the trip, I stand in front of Lincoln's birthplace, the small, one-room cabin in which his mother birthed him in 1809.

The log cabin is essential to Lincoln the myth; it's his manger and his she-wolf. Tourists lean forward over the railing, trying to aim their cameras into the room they can't actually enter. I walk around it over and over, circling it the way I circled his tomb, the way Honey circled the stage, trying to connect the beginning to the end.

In the cavernous space, the park ranger's voice bounces off the high ceiling as she recites the facts. At the turn of the century, the cabin was dismantled and reconstructed dozens of times as it toured the country, until a group of citizens, headed by Robert Collier of *Collier's Weekly* and including Samuel Gompers, William Jennings Bryan, and Mark Twain, purchased it in 1905. The group formed the Lincoln Farm Association the next year and raised $350,000 toward the construction of the monument in which the cabin now stands.

The echoes of the ranger's voice still ring softly while I look at the cabin. I wonder what piece I am looking at now. Was it originally a roof beam? Did it hold the wall together? Was this the beam that ran above the cabin's one window?

Like the spot where Lincoln delivered his speech in Michigan, the cabin has changed completely. Everything is different now. What matters is the monument, the frame that literally surrounds this structure and deems this spot, this cabin, this tomb to be important, when, in fact, it's just as common as any other.

I'll give you a hint about the cabin: *just as common.*

The monument is history. Everything else is unreliable.

AT THE CLUB CALLED DÉJÀ VU

She rocks her hips side to side, still facing away from us. Briefly, I wonder how she will take tips from us without underwear until I see the other men lining the stage with their dollars, and I follow suit. I wish that I could see Honey's face, of all things, right now. I wonder if she's smiling, aware of the trance she has all the men under. I wonder if she can feel all the energy in the room focused upon her and if that makes her nervous, or pleased, or something else entirely.

I'm naïve, of course. She is thinking of her rent, of how to make it through another night of this, of the pain in her ankles. I do not think of this. I want my Lincoln, my Honey. I avoid the definite article. I use the possessive.

And when she turns around, all the men's eyes drop to see the final revelation, to see her nearly hairless mons, just the thin strip marking her as woman, to see the small tattoo of a cherry that she has kept hidden all this time, to see her expose everything, her hands roaming over breasts and buttocks and crotch. In the brief moment before my eyes join those of the others, I see the look on her face. It is one of wonderment and history, of permanence and revision, a protean face ready to mimic whatever we need her to mimic for us, ready to mimic what she knows we need her to mimic for us.

Because she is the monument, and when making her rounds, collecting tips, she finishes her time in front of me by leaning in and kissing me softly on the cheek, I believe it, despite everything, despite all the unreliability. Honey's kiss, here in a strip club in Springfield, Illinois, a few miles away from where Lincoln lived and made his name and lies somewhere close to a red marble marker, is the most honest thing I have felt in a long time. And it is, most assuredly, a lie.

ON THE CEMETERY LAWN

I have believed in monuments, and I have believed in a stripper's kiss.

The morning after Honey's dance, I stand far away from the tomb, trying to fit it into the viewfinder of my camera. A few months from now, when I get the film back from the developer, I'll notice that I have taken almost the exact same photo as the one on the front of the brochure the Illinois Historic Preservation Society distributes: the obelisk, the base with the four statues at the corners, the ring building, the statue of the president, the name in high relief out of the Massachusetts granite. All of them from the same angle.

Months from now, after I have visited Springfield and Kalamazoo and Hodgenville, after I have driven through towns named after him and down streets named after him, past high schools and grade schools and city parks, I will turn all of this over in my mind. What did I see this summer that was real? What showed me Lincoln the man and not Lincoln the myth? What showed me *the* Lincoln and not *my* Lincoln?

I'll check out a book of Lincoln's collected writings this summer and imagine that I am fascinated with them, but eventually I'll slide it into the library's night return having read only a few speeches and letters. I pretend an obsession with Lincoln, but what I'm really obsessed with is his cult, with the Victorians who built a shrine to him in Springfield and the Americans who built a temple for him in Hodgenville, with Collier and Twain and Bryan and Gompers and the rest of the Lincoln Farm Association, with the Illinois Historic Preservation Society, with the tourists snapping pictures, with pilgrims and fetishists, and with myself.

Let me hear the myth of Lincoln without the complications of time. Let me believe that he was born here, that he spoke here, that his bones lie here, because none of those things matter as much as the way we remember him as our national hero, as the preserver of the Union, as Honest Abe. I know that the monuments create a reality the same way that Honey's kiss created a relationship that never existed, and ultimately I don't care.

AT THE CLUB CALLED DÉJÀ VU

Her second song fades out, and the DJ comes over the sound system, announcing the next dancer. With no music, Honey seems awkward as she sweeps the bills on the stage into a pile, grabbing them with one hand while she reaches for the discarded pieces of her clothing with the other. She is still nude, and yet our desire for her has vanished.

She sits on the steps to the stage and puts her clothes back on, the reverse of her earlier performance with a far smaller audience. Most of the men in the club have moved on, focusing their attentions to the newest dancer. If time worked differently, I would think of the tourists I have not yet seen, leaning over the rail to take photographs of Lincoln's cabin.

She stacks the dollars, folds them over, and puts them in a small purse, already bulging with money. Her face is expressionless.

IN THE BROCHURE (HODGENVILLE)

There are steps at the site; use caution.

When crossing roads be alert.

Stay on trails to avoid poison ivy, briars, ticks, and venomous snakes. Lock your vehicles and store possessions out of sight.

Please stay off the walls alongside the Memorial Building steps, as well as the walls at Sinking Spring, Boundary Oak, and the Plaza Area.

AT THE CLUB CALLED DÉJÀ VU

So she is gone, moved away like Lincoln's casket underneath the earth.

When the summer ends, months from now, what will the men who were in Springfield tonight remember of Honey? Will they remember the way she walked across the stage, the way she untied the knots holding her top on? Will they even remember what they came to see, her breasts, her buttocks, the thin strip?

What will we remember without help? What would we agree on in August about her?

The red marble and not the casket. The plaque and not the ground. The brochure and not the site. The temple. The cabin. The memorial. The monument.

IN CONCLUSION (LINCOLN'S LAST WRITING)

April 14, 1865
Allow Mr. Ashmun and friend to come in at 9 A.M. tomorrow.
A. Lincoln

IN CONCLUSION (MY LAST WRITING)

Allow me to come in and finish the work I am in.

The ranger in Hodgenville told me a secret, an open one, but she practically whispered it so that the other tourists in the memorial couldn't hear it and have their idea of Lincoln's origins disappointed. The National Park Service has dated the wood of the cabin. And they found that the trees were cut down sometime in the 1820s, which means that there's no way the cabin that stands protected by the memorial at the Abraham Lincoln Birthplace National Historical Site can be the true birthplace of Abraham Lincoln. The cabin that traveled the country, the cabin that Collier bought, is just a cabin, not *the* cabin.

The wood that surrounded Lincoln at his birth has rotted back into the soil that it grew out of, or went up some Kentuckian's chimney, or became part of the wall of some other cabin. But the monument in Hodgenville, the 1909 marble memorial with one step for each year of Lincoln's life makes its cabin Lincoln's, transforms common wood and pitch into the birthplace of a hero, as reliable as a statue's stone.

At Hodgenville, and at Kalamazoo and Springfield, and everywhere else, we agree upon a fiction that we call our history. We feel the story's lips brush our cheeks, and we agree to believe. The monument makes history.

The last thing Lincoln wrote was a memo, a piece of ephemera that would have been ignored if not for timing; it's not the grand summation of a life lived—not anything that would have contributed to his myth. It's simple and straightforward and dull, and I'd much rather think about any of his memorials than his last letter. I've chosen to let it fade back into the pages of his collected letters. Let the story of *my* Lincoln overwhelm the evidence of *the* Lincoln. Allow the monument to become the history. Believe in the kiss on my cheek. Believe the words on the plaque at my feet. Because if we relied on facts instead of stories, we'd never know where to stand; never know where our heroes were born or where they lie buried; never know where we were or where we are.

A for Accident

The car runs the light and comes directly for my door. True to cliché, time slows, enough that I can think, *He's going to hit us,* before he does, shoving my car off the road and toward a light pole. Time crawls for that second.

With a detachment that must emerge as a defense mechanism as we realize our imminent death, I watch the light pole coming toward us and think, *Shit, it would really be bad if we hit that. I hope we don't.*

My car stops about a foot in front of the pole. There is a brief moment—a second? a minute?—in which I realize that I haven't died, that no one will mark this light pole with a homemade cross and plastic flowers.

I turn to the girl I believe will be with me forever and say her name, ask if she's OK. She doesn't respond.

I ask again. Her head hangs down a little; I cannot see past her hair. She still doesn't reply.

Five years from now, I will live in a town where I've learned to count to three before proceeding when a light turns green, because so many drivers there run red lights. I will drive myself mad by thinking of how many accidents I avoid by taking one route over another, how many times I miss disaster simply by turning a block earlier.

Once I began looking for monuments and memorials, I found them everywhere: small brass historical markers on the sides of buildings, odd "in memory of" stickers on car windows, surprisingly enduring crosses at the side of the roads, at the sites of fatal car accidents. I walked down the road alongside the Black Warrior River and passed some that had been in place for years, still marking the loss.

I say the name of the girl I believe will be with me forever again, panic rising. "Are you OK?"

"Yeah," she says weakly, turning to look at me. Later she will tell me that she'd screamed so loudly when the car hit us that she couldn't talk. I hadn't heard her at all.

As we drive back in a rental car, a few hours after the accident, I think, *Tell her you love her.* We have been dating, or almost dating—no terms have been set—for a little while now, and yet I am convinced of our inevitability. I feel as though this accident can only bring us closer together, that our brush with death must unite us somehow.

I don't tell her that I love her. After I drop her off, I go home, undress, and find a round wound on my shin, sticky with blood, from where my leg must have hit the car's interior paneling. It is not far from the scar left by my old surgery, a new wound next to an old one, a dot next to a dash, a letter *A* upon my leg, written in Morse code on the body.

A few weeks after the accident, the girl I believe will be with me forever tells me that she had reunited with her ex-fiancé not long before we'd gone on the trip. She hadn't wanted to disappoint me, she said, and although she had technically cheated on him with me during our trip, she still wanted to be with him.

I had hoped that the wound wouldn't scar over, that I wouldn't have a reminder of that. I tended to the wound, coating it with antibiotic lotion and regularly changing the bandages. But it scarred, and it still shows no signs of fading, a memorial to an event that should have united us but ended up dividing us.

This Day in History

September 10, 1776: Nathan Hale volunteers to spy for the Continental Army.

* * *

I've been to New York City once in thirty-five years, so it's a little odd for me to presume that I could write anything about what to do with Ground Zero, or to critique what has been done with the site. I never saw the World Trade Center, except

> We will start with the palm (hollow of the hand), which holds the City of New York in detail (the twin towers, a statute of Mayor Giuliani, firefighters, etc) and is encased with the Pentagon as a base with a seagull at the top corner. The White House is engraved in the front of the base with the U.S. flag. All of the armed forces are represented. (entry 683975)

on television or in photographs, and it was on television and in photographs that I watched it destroyed.

I remember that when I saw the South Tower drop, I thought, *Well, they could probably rebuild one of them,* and when the North Tower fell, I was watching C-SPAN (though by that point every channel was the same), and they didn't say anything about it as it happened. A caller was going on about something—I don't remember what—and they didn't stop him.

* * *

September 10, 1913: The Lincoln Highway, America's first coast-to-coast highway, opens.

* * *

I have a joke: I lived in Manhattan for four years, but—wait for it—it was Manhattan, Kansas, which bills itself as "The Little Apple." Seriously. I guess if Anderson Hall on the campus of Kansas State University were attacked and destroyed, I might have an idea for what to do for a memorial, or at least feel more attached to what was built there.

When I've been close enough to New York City to see highway signs for it, I've been surprised as though I've seen a sign that reads "Mars: 250 miles." The city feels that remote to me. Television and movies don't really endear me to the town. It frustrates me with its omnipresence, how everything's set there, how everything seems to revolve around it, and how it sometimes mocks where I'm from, something about a flyover state or a Toto joke.

* * *

September 10, 1945: Vidkun Quisling is sentenced to die for collaborating with the Nazis in Norway.

* * *

I'd guess, though, that a lot of the people who submitted designs for the WTC memorial have never been to NYC either. I mean, 5,201 submissions is a lot. And not all of them are by certified architects; there are entries with bad grammar, freehand drawings, and handwritten descriptions.

> The garden of peace could be in one section or in two sections on either side of the walkway of the river of peace. The unidentified remains may be put in this contemplation area. The walk can include a walkway with peace in many languages engraved in the stones—for example, peace—U.S.A., shalom —Israel, etc. Benches and seating places would be apparent throughout the garden, as well as weeping willows, weeping cherry trees and flowering trees such as crabapple and red bud, etc. to depict hope. The area would be surrounded by many varieties of the peace rose to go with the theme of the garden of peace as well as other appropriate plants and bushes. (entry 683984)

I find it difficult to remember what it felt like that day. I remember it was nice outside. I remember my clock radio woke me up with the news of the second tower being hit. I remember turning on the television, flipping through the channels as they all interrupted their coverage, ending up on C-SPAN for no reason at all. I remember being grateful to find a coffee shop that afternoon that didn't have its television on. I remember seeing a man walking down the street, carrying an American flag, and flashing the peace sign to honking cars. That seems odd now.

* * *

September 10, 1990: Iran and Iraq resume diplomatic ties.

> The Garden of the Moment takes the idealized form of the footprint of the tower that once stood in its place. The charred, bent and deformed outer shell wraps the garden. Most of the footprint has an open lawn, except in the location of its former core which contains fractured columns, and stairs which took so many to safety, now standing as sculptural elements. Within the area that was the core are four large pylons each evoking some aspect of the moment. The first encases a flame eternal and powerful. The second, billowing smoke and everlasting darkness. The Third contains objects of daily life thrown to the wind, bills, pictures, and memos swirling around in a vortex. The final Pylon contains video and still images a simple representation of how this event was tied to the world and the world to this spot. (entry 683610)

* * *

And this is the trouble with trying to build a memorial for what happened, with trying to fix that moment in time: so much history has accrued, even in the short time since. When I visited the Flight 93 crash site in Shanksville, we weren't in Iraq yet. Now September 11 and the Iraq war seem impossibly linked, one as the excuse for the other.

> The central theme for this proposed memorial design is the individual recognition of each and every victim at the site. A sculptor will be commissioned to create a likeness of each person's face out of stone or bronze. Each face will be shown in relief within a uniform sized block. (Approximately one foot square per block.) The name, place of birth and birthday for each victim will be inscribed on the block. (entry 683256)

* * *

Every day is history.

* * *

Every day is ordinary.

* * *

September 10, 1919: General John J. Pershing and 25,000 soldiers are welcomed with a parade in New York City.

* * *

For instance, my birthday. March 25 probably passes unnoticed for you each year, but for me it's a significant date. If you're Catholic, you know it's the Annunciation. If you're a history buff, you know it's the anniversary of the Triangle Shirtwaist Factory fire.

> The footprint of the South Tower is marked by a granite enclosure that rises above the height of the upper street level. It is a brooding, anonymous object, whose gravity is evident by the canted walls that loom over visitors. The entry is marked by a modest slot that is sliced through the black granite face. Set in front of the waterfall, this enclosure acts to contain the power of the rushing water: a sound barrier between the tower footprint and the rest of the memorial site. Within, it becomes an amphitheater—a series of concentric steps of black granite radiating upwards from a 50' by 50' central plaza. In contrast to one's initial perception, as one climbs the steps to the top, each row of stairs reveals itself to be inset with grass, invisible to visitors from below. Each grass face provides a comfortable seating area for individuals to contemplate the sight and sound of the waterfall. (entry 122599)

But for most people, March 25 is just twenty-four hours of their lives, the regular twists and turns of daily existence.

But this event, the one we're trying to memorialize, it happened to all of us. Whether it interrupted our morning or greeted us when we woke, we watched it, gravitating toward television screens, then, in disbelief, gravitating toward each other, trying to make something out of what we had witnessed.

* * *

September 10, 1955: *Gunsmoke* premieres on CBS.

* * *

And we saw it happen. Now I don't see it much; it's like it has gone from the specific act to a remembered date. I find it odd each year to see the footage again on the anniversaries, the moments of impact, the collapse, the sudden remembering of that single day.

* * *

In 2006, on CNN's website, visitors could watch the live footage from that morning five years earlier, as it happened. The anchors take a long time to realize what's happening. Even after the second plane hits, they still theorize that maybe it's an air traffic navigation malfunction. There's not a little denial and disbelief at work in their voices. For me, watching it five years later, I felt only regret and sorrow, both for the day and for what I knew would follow.

* * *

September 10, 1608: John Smith becomes president of the Jamestown colony in Virginia.

* * *

Each of us started out somewhere and ended up somewhere else, and looking back it's difficult to remember how we felt when we started. I haven't lived in Kansas for over a decade. I don't remember what it's like to be there.

> The chime tower and the display of individual photographs are meant to emphasize the uniqueness of each person. The chime tower will use music to symbolize the victims' spirits that will always live on in the lives of their loved ones. The chime tower will play uniquely created music as well as provide a special type of visual physical representation of the huge number of lives lost. The tower displays 3,022 chimes (one for each victim), each with a unique design (color and shape) and with each producing a unique sound. (entry 122134)

* * *

So many of the design proposals submitted for the contest discuss the desire for the memorial to heal the country, to relieve the suffering they ascribe to all of us, but especially to the victims' families.

* * *

> The remainder of the site is entirely paved with limestone and no landscaping is added to define this subterranean urban space. The memorial is one that emphasizes the sheer volume of senseless murders achieved during these acts of terrorism. The scale and detailing fill but do not overwhelm the site and keep the proportions on a manageable human dimension. Hopefully, this serene and uncomplicated design will heal a grieving nation. (entry 446243)

September 10, 1924: A jury declares Leopold and Loeb guilty of murder.

* * *

There's a frequently expressed wish to bring the nation back together, to halt time at the point when we were still together, before everything fell apart, before we lost the way. And either they're idealizing the time before September 11, as fractious and divided as any other, or they're idealizing the days immediately after, the not-quite-month before we invaded Afghanistan. They're remembering the flags waving from what seemed like every house; they're remembering the lines of Americans waiting to donate blood. That's a difficult project for a memorial—trying to bring the country back to a time that barely existed, that maybe never existed. After all, the Red Cross, overwhelmed with donations, threw out thousands of gallons of blood that they couldn't store. And the competition placed so many restrictions on the memorial's design—it must preserve the footprints of the towers, it must feature a space for unidentified remains, it must feature a private space for the victims' families—that to add "unify the country" to the to-do list seems a little optimistic.

The site itself rebels against being fixed in time. Workers in 2006, opening some manholes for the first time since the attack, found human remains. Like a Civil War battlefield, the World Trade Center still holds its dead close to itself.

I keep thinking about paper memorials: the posters of the missing plastering the walls of New York City, the special editions of newspapers with their 120-point headlines. Most of all, I keep thinking about the paper that fell from the sky that day, ephemera of corporate life burned at the edges. I keep thinking about how in a stockholder report, a blank page is never blank, never empty; instead, at the bottom, small type announces, *This page intentionally left blank.*

* * *

The void acknowledged, the absence felt. In 2001 I had never been to New York City, but I nevertheless felt sorrow and fear that day. I felt sorrow and fear that day, but I hide that now.

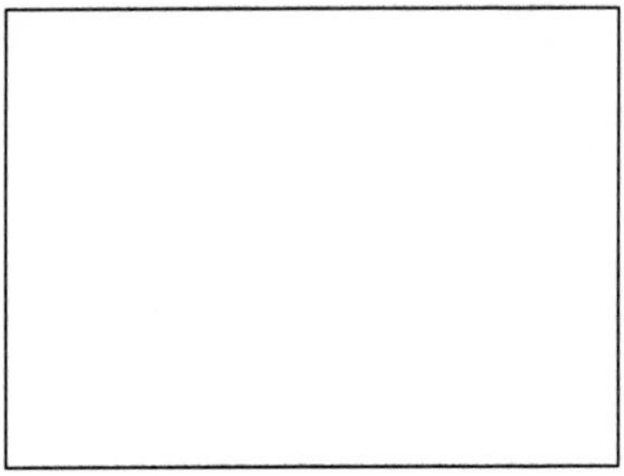

* * *

September 10, 1734: British clergyman George Whitefield writes, "Pain, if patiently endured, and sanctified to us, is a great purifier of our corrupted nature."

* * *

A lot of the proposals don't make much sense.

* * *

September 10, 1981: Picasso's *Guernica* returns to Spain.

* * *

The design concept starts from the statue of liberty, drawing an imagery line from liberty to the site with 2 lines of **lights**. Reaching to the site the lights turn into **water—*a symbol of light, innocent and life***—then a **waterfall** will guide the water down to the ground Zero, which the **wall** holding the water fall will serve as a separate accessible space to serve as a final resting-place for the unidentified remains from the World Trade Center site. In the lower level there is a **wide space** surrounding water which serves as an space for contemplation. in the continuing of the water is the **frame,** *the frame contains the name of the victims on it's body* and is holding the American **flag painting** that stand high, it is a symbol of 2 towers who are united on top. The tall frame holds the painting—both site of the plate contain the same painting—that represent an original and powerful statement of enduring and unifying symbolism. (entry 350023)

* * *

Which might be a legitimate response.

* * *

My favorite proposal is one that I heard just a few days afterward. Tear it all down, the artist said, level it off and plant native grasses. Establish a bison herd on the site, restoring some of what once was to the commotion of lower Manhattan. I like this because it takes the impulse to push the clock back to its

We decided that the remains should not be relegated to some corner, but made the gravitational center of the memorial. That is what matters; it is the lives that made this place sacred. Thus we envisioned a single, central grave extending along one side of the north-tower footprint to the opposite side of the south-tower footprint. Beneath the line would be buried the unidentified remains. (entry 089005) logical extreme: remove human involvement from the site. Humans did this to other humans; the best way to memorialize the site, to honor the victims, is to return to the time before humans harmed other humans. It is to write, in a way, *This site intentionally left blank.*

* * *

September 10, 1939: Canada declares war on Germany.

* * *

As far as I know, that proposal was never officially submitted. And probably for good reason; even when there were only four people on Earth, one of them was a murderer and one of them was a victim.

When someday I visit the National September 11 Memorial and Museum in New York City, dedicated on the tenth anniversary of the attacks, I will peer into the curtain of water and at the ribbon of names, and running my hand over the engraved letters, spelling out one of thousands of names, I will see history fixed in place. I will tell my family—a family that does not exist as I write this, on this day in history—about how I woke up to my clock radio's news, how I watched the towers fall live on television. I will tell them how I felt that day, and in the months and years afterward, how the event changed with other events, each one's gravitational pull affecting the other. We will watch the water fall, disappearing into the preserved abyss of the footprints, and maybe I will be reminded of the towers falling. Maybe I will be reminded of fifty-two hundred unbuilt memorials.

> Bordering each pool is a pair of ramps that lead down to the memorial spaces. Descending into the memorial, visitors are removed from the sights and sounds of the city and immersed in a cool darkness. As they proceed, the sound of water falling grows louder, and more daylight filters in from below. At the bottom of the descent, they find themselves behind a thin curtain of water, staring out into an enormous pool. Surrounding this pool is a continuous ribbon of names. The enormity of this space and the multitude of names that form this endless ribbon underscore the vast scope of the destruction. Standing there at the water's edge, looking at a pool of water that is flowing away into an abyss, a visitor to the site can sense that what is beyond this curtain of water and ribbon of names is inaccessible. (winning entry)

Maybe I will remember how one day in college, driving outside the Little Apple, I came upon a field of bison. Several stood next to the fence's gate, quietly grazing. I parked my car nearby and walked toward them, trying not to scare the animals. As I approached, they did not move away, and I found myself face-to-face with a single bison, with only the bars of the gate between us. I looked into the bison's eye. I wanted to see history, the billions of bison that once roamed the entire continent. I wanted to see the power that I knew dwelled in the bison's enormous frame. I wanted to see survival, the continuation of a species that man almost destroyed.

I wanted to see all of these things, but on that day in Kansas, quiet and sunny, when I looked into the bison's eye, I saw only a single glassy black orb in which I could see nothing reflected.

Doors

Spring came to Tuscaloosa last Monday, a brief two-week season between the forty-degree winter and too-humid summer, and the trees have all blossomed. I can't see any of that, though. When I look around the building I'm in, Foster Auditorium, the only thing I find is all the proof of its neglect and decay: paint peeling off the walls, falling onto the dusty floor. Loose ceiling tiles wobble precariously as air barely circulates around the room. All the doors, except the one I've just walked through, have heavy chains and locks around them, and two orange bars form a cross on the top of each basketball hoop, keeping them from play.

If I'd attended the University of Alabama forty years earlier, I would have come to register for my classes here in Foster Auditorium. Now I'm not here to do anything but look around, which is pretty much all anyone does with Foster anymore, since no one seems to know what to do with a building with a history.

* * *

All the history of Foster Auditorium can be reduced down to a single day, June 11, 1963, when Governor George Wallace, fulfilling the promise he'd made in his inaugural speech that January, attempted to block two black students from enrolling for the summer session and thereby integrating the university. Nicholas Katzenbach, acting as the official representative of the Kennedy administration, and with the backing of the federalized Alabama National Guard, ordered Wallace to stand aside and allow Vivian Malone and James Hood to enter the building and enroll.

Wallace acquiesced, and the moment became another victory for the civil rights movement, the latest in a long string of successes that had started only a short drive down the highway in Montgomery, where Martin Luther King Jr. had led the boycott of the bus system eight years earlier.

After the integration of the University of Alabama, the civil rights movement experienced other, bigger events: the March on Washington and the "I Have a Dream" speech, Freedom Summer '64 and the murder of three civil rights workers in Mississippi, the march from Montgomery to Selma, the passage of the Civil Rights Act and the Voting Rights Act. The spotlight shifted away from Tuscaloosa and the university. Foster Auditorium remained, marked by the events that had taken place in front of it for a few hours on a hot June day in 1963.

* * *

I want to register for three classes—two for my graduate program, and one just for fun, or, I guess, something a fifth-year graduate student would think was fun. I meet with my advisor, and we talk about what I need to do to earn enough credits to graduate, which gaps I need to fill in with which classes. She gives me the numbers I need to register. There are new ways to register now, including online and on the phone. None of the methods require me to go anywhere particular. None of the methods requires a building.

* * *

Forty years after Wallace stepped aside for Malone and Hood, Foster Auditorium is a footnote on campus, almost completely abandoned and unnoticed by the student body. Other sites at the university are more prominent, like the president's mansion, an antebellum home, and the remains of Franklin Hall, buried under a mound after the Union Army burned it down along with most of the campus in the waning days of the Civil War. And of course there is the football stadium, a great god visible all over town that watches over the campus.

Foster Auditorium isn't on the campus tour for freshmen, nor are there any signs that might lead a tourist to it from the main streets as there are for the Paul W. Bryant Museum. The only proof of its role as a setting in the civil rights movement is a medium-size plaque next to the door Wallace blocked, carefully worded to avoid upsetting and offending any group:

SITE OF THE STAND
IN THE SCHOOLHOUSE DOOR
FOSTER AUDITORIUM IS THE SITE OF THE JUNE 11, 1963,
"STAND IN THE SCHOOLHOUSE DOOR"
by
Governor George C. Wallace
in defiance of a court order requiring The University of Alabama
to admit African-American students Vivian Malone and James Hood.
President John F. Kennedy placed the Alabama National Guard
under federal control to enforce the court order
as Wallace refused to obey. Wallace then stepped aside
and the students registered for class.
That night, President Kennedy went on television to declare civil rights
no longer simply a legal issue but a moral issue
and appealed to the nation's sense of fairness.
One week later, he submitted a comprehensive civil rights bill
that became the foundation of the Civil Rights Act of 1964.

Sixty-five years after it was built, Foster Auditorium, for many of those years a functioning facility for the University of Alabama—the place where the basketball team played, the place where touring acts played, the place where thousands of students registered for classes—has been reduced to a door and a marker, a monument with a giant empty building attached to it.

* * *

When I was an undergraduate at Kansas State University, another large state school, registration took place in the chemistry building, a hall I never went to except for those two times a year when we signed up for our classes. We registered based on how many credit hours we'd obtained, seniors and juniors signing up before sophomores and freshmen.

When, after reaching the front of the line that snaked up and down the hall, I would reach the registration room, I would sit down at a table with an elderly woman (strangely, all the people who did the actual act of registration were elderly women, whose connection to the university I never understood), who would enter my class numbers into a computer and confirm the openings in the classes I wanted to take.

That system, that group experience made up of individuals, is gone now. Like most every other school, Kansas State does its registration for classes online now.

* * *

At the fortieth anniversary of the marking event, the president of the university assures concerned parties that, despite its near-vacant status, Foster Auditorium will not be torn down. He tells them that he is committed to forming an administrative unit that will focus on multiculturalism and that it will be called either the Office of Multicultural Affairs or the Office of Diversity and Inclusiveness. He tells them that he is asking Malone and Hood, among others, to be on the advisory committee. He tells them that he plans to submit Foster Auditorium as a candidate for National Historic Landmark status, which would mean it would be preserved forever. He tells them that he would love to see the building renovated into a multicultural center.

Behind the president's mansion are three buildings generally believed to have served as slave quarters. On the campus somewhere are the unmarked graves of slaves owned by the university itself. He tells the concerned parties that he plans to memorialize those as well. The trouble is that there is so little money available for a project of the magnitude of renovating Foster. Later the graves will have been found and marked, and the slave quarters will be pointed out to tourists who know enough to ask, but Foster Auditorium will still be empty, alone with years of dust that has blown in through broken window panes and underneath Wallace's door.

* * *

What registration is—more so than actually attending classes, or studying, or anything we might regard as the real core of attending college—is the moment when the student is recognized as an individual human being by the university and, by extension, the state and society. Wallace blocked Malone and Hood not from entering the classroom, but from establishing their identities officially, from forcing the state to admit their humanity. Think of the famous signs carried in the Memphis sanitation workers' strike: "I am a man," not "I am a worker." If Malone and Hood wanted to be students, they could have entered the classroom. What they wanted was to be real in the eyes of the government, and to become that, they needed to enter Foster Auditorium.

* * *

In 1956, after the Supreme Court ordered the desegregation of public schools, Autherine Lucy integrated the University of Alabama for the first time. On the third day of classes, as she left Smith Hall, she was taunted and jeered at by students, townspeople, and people from out of town, who threw rocks and eggs at her and her police escort. The university promptly suspended her, declaring they could not guarantee her safety, and later expelled her for claiming, through her lawyers, that the suspension was racially motivated.

While Malone and Hood became known as the first students to integrate the university, Lucy is the true first, the tentative foray into making history. A combination of national and state politics, a civil rights movement not yet as confident and assured as it would eventually become, and a fully segregated university system throughout the South turned her into a footnote, a forgotten chapter of a school's history and a movement's failings.

Smith Hall now holds the Department of Geological Sciences, and students file in and out of it all day long. In their offices, professors work on whatever their latest projects are. Something happened outside of Smith Hall in 1956, but history did not deem it important enough to put a plaque there, to set it aside for future generations to observe as a relic of its time. History has not turned it into a vacant building. History, in its forgetting, has kept it alive.

* * *

Every student became real in the eyes of the establishment at the moment of registration. The careful construction of the schedule, the checking and rechecking of the lists of closed classes, the waiting in the endless lines, and, finally, the reception of the confirmed schedule: all this was, for each individual student, his or her moment of recognition by the university.

In this computer age, when I can register for my classes at home or in the car or in a coffee shop, what do I lose by not going through that in-person process? What did the interminable line preserve that the phone line abandoned?

* * *

Foster Auditorium is not completely abandoned. There are a few offices there, mostly faculty in a small department that has its main office in another, newer building. When these people pass through the building, they appear like strangely real figures in a ghostly landscape, surprising and obtrusive.

One day, finding me standing in the middle of an empty basketball court, one of the faculty members tells me a story. Every year, he says, on June 10, landscaping crews come and beautify the front façade of Foster. They wash the dirt off of the yellow brick, shine up the plaque, and plant flowers in the beds, red and white ones for the university's colors. On the eleventh, the president of the university, the provosts and deans, the administrators, the press, and various people the university wants to impress arrive. They give speeches in which they declaim their support for diversity at the school and express their unswerving commitment to multiculturalism. They reenact Wallace's stand, but this time they open their arms to minority students, rewriting history and erasing the sins of the past.

They do all of this, the faculty member tells me, and then the very next day, the landscaping crews come back and pull the flowers out of the beds, load them back into their trucks, and drive them away. They undo the beautification of two days before, the effect of the single day each year when Foster Auditorium finds itself in the present instead of simply a memorial of the past.

"I imagine that if they knew how to put the dirt back on the walls, they would," the faculty member says, ending his story, and he vanishes into the hallways of the building.

* * *

The act of registration is so powerful that it can create a real person out of nothing, like God forming Adam out of the dust of the prelapsarian Eden. Take the case, possibly apocryphal, of the four students at a Midwestern university, who, in the days of punch cards, managed to register a fictional student. They took turns taking his classes, passing his tests, and, four years later, graduated him with a degree in economics. Now, almost thirty years later, this unreal alumnus receives reunion notices and solicitations for donations in the post office box that his four creators still maintain.

No wonder Wallace wanted to block Malone and Hood from passing through the door of Foster Auditorium. The creative act of registration would have given the idea of the African American scholar far more reality, far more equality in the public sphere than almost any other action. It's one thing to earn the same wage, to ride in the same section of the bus, and another entirely to have the same legal, official status as the great-grandchildren of slave owners, to sit next to them in a classroom and stand in front of them in the registration line.

* * *

We all focus on the door: Wallace's door that could not be opened without the intervention of the federal government, Malone and Hood's door that was closed to them for so long, the door by which the carefully worded plaque has been installed, the door that is cleaned off every year for the dignitaries to pose in front of. We focus on the door and only the door, and never the passage from the door into the auditorium.

Not far from the door into Foster Auditorium, a second Alabama door holds its place in history. In the Birmingham Civil Rights Institute, the cell door behind which Martin Luther King Jr. wrote his "Letter from Birmingham Jail," a plain iron door stands. If you visit it, you can look right through it, can reach out and touch the bars worn smooth. There is no inside/outside to this door, no mystery lying behind it. Because what gave this door history occurred behind it, we must look through the door to understand it.

The history of the Foster Auditorium door, however, comes from what took place in front of it. To enter the building is unnecessary, perhaps even discouraged, because the building itself has become unnecessary.

* * *

Once inside Foster Auditorium, among the bleachers and orange hoops, the same hoops that I find locked forty years later, what would Malone and Hood have found? The important part, the door, stands behind them; in front of them is the regulated order of school registration.

Imagine a gymnasium filled with students, the air stifling in the Alabama summer. Everyone waits in line, papers in hand perhaps, patiently moving toward a table where they pay their tuition or collect their scholarships. It's not the most exciting of scenarios inside the building; it certainly doesn't lend itself to a heroic mural or interpretive exhibit. All the drama is on the outside.

* * *

How, then, should we make Foster Auditorium necessary? What place should we give the building in the history of university integration? After all, Alabama was the last state to integrate its schools, holding out after all the other strongholds had crumbled in the face of lawsuits and federal marshals. Foster Auditorium was not the key battle, but rather the final surrender of the old guard.

How do we judge a site's historical importance? No one died at the University of Alabama as two had when Ole Miss had been integrated the year before, when Governor Ross Barnett called the Kennedy administration's actions an "invasion" of his state.

Must blood be spilled, tempers flared, epithets shouted and stones thrown to justify a monument? In the time between Ole Miss and Alabama's confrontations, South Carolina's Clemson University was peacefully integrated, an eye in the middle of the South's stormy realignment of itself, and it, like Autherine Lucy, has been relegated to minor importance by the historians.

Then, finally, the sheer number of sites in this region defies our ability to preserve the past. If we were to mark every site where something occurred here, we should find ourselves surrounded by plaques and markers, crowded into a forest of memory. If history removes utility, this whole region would quickly become unusable.

Because of Spanish exploration and conquest, the South has the longest history of European and African presence in the United States. So much has happened here—exploration, expulsion and extermination of natives, the antebellum years, the Civil War, Reconstruction, the civil rights movement—that more than any other region the South has been forced to find a way to function despite all of its history.

Nothing ever dies in the South; it rarely freezes or snows, so plants grow lush and thick, overgrowing telephone poles, fences, entire buildings. This makes Foster Auditorium the perfect representative of Dixie and its history. It will not go away. It will not keep itself to an easily managed space. It will not disappear and become the past; instead it will leave uncomfortable reminders of its presence in our daily lives, wounds not fully healed, ghosts not completely vanished. We wish for a door and find ourselves stuck with an entire building, an unwanted memory.

* * *

Eventually, after all this rumination on registration, I call the phone registration line, and a mechanical voice walks me through the process: entering my campus-wide ID, followed by the individual numbers of each class that I wish to take. The campus-wide ID, an eight-digit code, replaced the usual Social Security number in the aftermath of a university election scandal a few years ago in which the numbers of several hundred students were stolen and used to vote for a particular candidate online. So now the University of Alabama's students find themselves in the odd situation of having a new number replace the old number by which they were known. We've exchanged one form of anonymity for another.

Punching the numbers into the touchtone phone, I think, *Anyone could do this. Anyone could be me.* How much fuss would be made if Malone and Hood could have phoned in their registration? What door could Wallace possibly have blocked to symbolize his opposition to integration? The door to Foster Auditorium would have simply stayed a door like any other, as anonymous as whoever's pressing the pound key to skip to the main menu.

* * *

One more door. In Memphis, at the site of the Lorraine Motel, a wreath hangs on the fence in front of the door to a second-story room. In April 1968, a little less than five years after Foster's door swung open, a single bullet killed Martin Luther King Jr. in front of this door, marking it for preservation.

And so it came, years later, when the Lorraine Motel was nearly closed and under consideration for demolition, that a group of citizens and investors stepped in, bought the building, and saved it. Now the former Lorraine Motel is the National Civil Rights Museum, an enormous facility that tracks the history of the movement from its beginnings to King's death. Its emotional climax comes at the room King stayed in the night before he died, the room he'd left just before he was shot. From behind Plexiglas windows, visitors can see into the room, see the bed and nightstand and the door through which King passed, unknowingly.

Across the street from the Lorraine Motel/National Civil Rights Museum stands the boardinghouse from which James Earl Ray supposedly fired the bullet. Toward the end of the century, this building faced development into luxury condominiums, and it too was purchased by the museum. It has been preserved and turned into a second museum, one that chronicles the assassination's aftermath—the investigation, the pursuit, the trial, even all the conspiracies.

It has saved all the evidence: Ray's fake passports, his registration card from the boardinghouse, his receipt for the rifle, and the rifle itself. Unremarkably placed in the middle of the evidence is a small, mangled bit of metal: the bullet.

Like King's room, the bathroom from which Ray fired is walled off with Plexiglas, so visitors cannot stand in front of it and see the balcony where King died. But they can stand in the street, outside of the buildings they must pay admission to enter, and see the reasons for the millions of dollars and thousands of hours of labor that have preserved and renovated these buildings.

A window, a door, and the path between the two.

* * *

I have walked away from Foster Auditorium, leaving it to the dust and cobwebs and the rocks that fly through the windows sometimes, spilling broken glass onto the unused parquet floor. I cross the street that runs alongside the building, walking toward the center of campus. On the fringes of the campus, construction workers build new structures, luxurious dormitories and classrooms with wireless access, residences designed to keep students living on campus for all four or five years of their time in Tuscaloosa.

Dust means one of two things: neglect or genesis. On the edges of campus, the dust kicked up by earthmovers and cranes symbolizes newness, the evolution of the college campus. But at Foster Auditorium, that vestigial organ of the university, the dust lies thick and undisturbed like the dust of a tomb, like the dust on top of a book unopened in this century.

* * *

In the summer of 2003, Bob Riley, the governor of Alabama, spoke at ceremonies commemorating the fortieth anniversary of the integration of the university. Both he and the previous speaker, Vivian Malone Jones, stood in the exact same spot where Wallace had stood forty years earlier. In the middle of his remarks, a summer thunderstorm let loose. The assembled group moved into the closest building in which they could find shelter, through the door into Foster Auditorium.

On the other side of the door, while technicians scrambled to set up the public address system, everyone found themselves in the forgotten part of Foster. They saw the dust, the broken windows up high, the pushed-in bleachers, and the basketball goals with rim locks fastened to each one. For a few hours, while Riley gave his speech and the ceremony concluded, Foster Auditorium lived again as a working facility instead of the empty monument it normally is, as something more than just a door. After the speeches, though, everyone left. And if the story the faculty member told me was true, the next day the landscape crews came and took out the flowers, and Foster Auditorium slipped back into history.

It's possible that one day the money will come through and Foster Auditorium will become the multicultural center that the school promises. It's possible that the cracked parquet floor, the bleachers, and the goals will be torn out and replaced by a gleaming new facility. It's possible that one day the building might be a place where people come to understand the struggle to integrate the schools of the South, to remember Ole Miss and Clemson and Alabama the way that King's life and death is remembered in Memphis.

But no one spends the night in the Lorraine Motel, and no one rents a room in the boardinghouse across the street from it. Just the same, no one will use the renovated Foster Auditorium for any of the thousand purposes that gave it its quotidian history, its history inside the door and outside of the door.

When the day comes that the governor and the president of the university preside over Malone and Hood, or perhaps Autherine Lucy, or perhaps some of their children, cutting the ribbon that opens the new Foster Auditorium Multicultural Center, the building will begin to accumulate its new history, a history of memory. But something will have been left out of the informative exhibits and self-guided tours; no band will ever play Foster again, no student will ever wait in line to register for classes, no team will ever sink a shot at the last second to win the game for Alabama.

This is the problem with preservation: something is always lost.

A for Accumulation

All of this scar tissue builds up until it's nearly impossible to penetrate. I'm careful, when I donate blood, to alternate arms, even though I have great veins, veins I'm complimented on, veins they call the trainees over to do. I don't want to have access blocked to this, one of the few good things I do regularly. The tiny needle pricks in the crooks of my arms are the few scars I can look at and remember fondly, feel good about having. They remind me, in my overdramatic moments, of the speech Shakespeare's Henry V gives to his troops before the battle of Agincourt: "He will strip his sleeves and show his scars / and say, 'These wounds I had on Crispin's day.'"

The needle pricks, the scars I have earned through my good deed and that I will continue to accumulate as long as I can, are the memorial I'm building upon myself, the moral right that

Minot Judson Savage must have meant when he wrote that man must be his own monument.

After all these travels, all this searching, all these monuments and memorials, I found myself wanting to remember my own self. There was a woman, Elizabeth, and she and I had found ourselves drawn together. She felt right, and real, in ways that none of the other women had. I wanted to stay with her, to rest in her.

I looked to my body to remember, and without tattoos I could find only the accidental scars to remind me of that time. We were both scarred; she had seen my leg, and I had grown fond of a thin scar on her hip, a reminder of a slip in the shower years before we met.

I had three candidates, still red and raw: a spot on the back of my left hand where I had backhanded the corner of a cabinet; the tip of my right index finger, which I had caught while chopping vegetables; and a thick strip across my right thumb where I had peeled off part of myself along with the zest of a lime.

All three of these injuries had occurred in the kitchen. We cooked together a lot, I think, because both of us came from relationships in which the other person had no appetite, ate the same things over and over. There is a danger inherent in the new, a risk of injury; this was why injuries from cooking covered my hands in those days.

At that time we lived in a nation torn by its self-inflicted traumas, a nation that tried to win without sacrifice, to do good without injury, and realized too late that even a good intention would leave a hole in the arm. We lived in a state that could not close its old wounds without opening new ones, and found itself scarred by its history. Some of those scars it chose to embrace and others it disdained.

I wanted something on my body from that time. Now, years later, it is that last wound, the strip on my right thumb, that has remained. It is a white line, nearly invisible, but when I see it, I remember the moments of Elizabeth and me cooking together, feeding each other what we had lacked, creating our lives together in her small apartment kitchen in Alabama. And the state, too, has tended to its wounds. The once-empty Foster Auditorium now stands at the center of the newly dedicated Malone-Hood Plaza, facing the Autherine Lucy Clock Tower.

Time heals all, but it is slow, and it leaves its mark. It is bad only when it reminds us of the bad.

What I Was Doing There

SATURDAY, AUGUST 2

Finding a crowded spot on the island of Oahu isn't hard. The island, home to Honolulu International Airport (upgrade your rental car to a convertible for just an extra five dollars a day!), contains the fiftieth state's largest city, most thoroughly equipped shopping mall, and the majority of its main tourist sites. Several experienced travel guides suggest using the island merely as a jumping-off point to the other islands in the Hawaiian chain. Your most important Oahu experience, they say, should be walking through the open-air terminals of HNL to catch your flight to Lanai or Molokai or some other, less-crowded island.

But Elizabeth and I are here to visit some crowded locations, to be tourists. Neither of us has visited Hawaii, and we want to see the sights. And already our trip has been beset by delays and aggravations—we spent the night two nights ago catching fitful naps on the floor of LAX, having missed our connecting flight from Atlanta thanks to a storm. After arriving yesterday, we drove straight to the Department of Health in downtown Honolulu, parked not far from the volcano-shaped capitol building, and waited for an hour on a Friday afternoon in molded plastic seats for a pleasant woman to ask us several questions, the answers recorded dutifully before she handed us our marriage license, ready just in time for our beachside ceremony on Monday morning.

Now it's Saturday, August 2, and we are standing in front of a snorkel rental shack on a beach inside a collapsed volcano's crater. We made sure to wake up early, to be in the parking lot right when the beach park opened. Still, as we wait for the shack's employees, more and more people trickle down the hill toward the water. By mid-morning this place will be packed with tourists, including us.

I suppose I should tell you where I am and what I am doing here. This is an essay about time, the ways we mark it, the ways we record it, the ways it changes our understanding of the universe and ourselves. And while we were on Oahu for ten days, doing all sorts of tourist/honeymoon activities (surfing lessons on the North Shore, couples massage at the Oriental Mandarin Spa), for this essay you need to be concerned about only three: August 2, 3, and 4. These three days passed as normal for billions of people around the world; for me, they contained multitudes.

And about me: I am from Kansas. My family considered a vacation to be driving twelve hours across the state and eastern Colorado to look at mountains. We hiked, we camped; sometimes we just walked around Boulder, where my parents had visited since their college days. The idea of the beach—thousands of miles in any direction from our house—seemed as foreign to me as the idea of vacationing on the moon.

Now, at age thirty-two, I'm getting married on the beach in Hawaii, with just Captain Howie, an officiant who's also a maritime captain, and Jenn and Jeremy, the two friends who flew here to stand with us, and no one else. We chose this sort of wedding because we wanted a ceremony that was about us, not about the masses of extended families and friends, or about us spending a lot of money that we didn't really have. Another reason, too: my wife's brother, who more than anyone else we would want at this event, cannot travel, because he is undergoing another surgery to try to repair the body shattered nine months earlier by a drunk driver. When we speak to him after the ceremony, he'll apologize for the timing of the operation, for making us worry about him on our wedding day.

My family has not taken my decision well. After berating me on the phone for thirty minutes, my father hasn't spoken to me in almost two months. My mother cries frequently, asks what she's supposed to tell everyone else. My sister tells me how selfish she thinks I am.

Maybe I am, and yet when I think about marrying Elizabeth, this is what I see happening: the two of us on a beach at sunrise, each holding the other's hand, and speaking the words that join us together.

After we have finished snorkeling at Hanauma Bay and have returned our fins and masks, when I take my phone from the car's glove box, I see the small envelope icon signifying that I have a voicemail from my parents. I do not want to listen to it, so I put the phone in my pocket, put the top down on our convertible, and drive off, back to Honolulu.

SUNDAY, AUGUST 3

Months earlier, a stack of guidebooks in front of us, we had made a list of the places we wanted to visit while in Oahu. Elizabeth set down a book and sighed.

"OK, we should go to Pearl Harbor while we're there, right?" she said. "But we should go before Monday so that we don't technically go there while we're on our honeymoon."

"If that's the case," I say, "we could also go to the National Memorial Cemetery of the Pacific the same day. It's supposed to be beautiful—it's in an extinct volcano crater. Didion mentions it in her Hawaii essay."

Joan Didion's "In the Islands," written between 1969 and 1977, is one of my favorite essays by one of my favorite authors. While we've been planning our honeymoon—and the days in Hawaii before our wedding—I've been thinking a lot about her essay, its famous opening line ("I had better tell you where I am, and why"), the portrait it sketches of a marriage in quiet crisis, waiting for a possible tsunami to strike the beach at the Royal Hawaiian Hotel. I think often of the way Didion describes herself as "a woman who for some time now has felt radically separated from most of the ideas that seem to interest other people."

That description has echoed in me these last few years. I've dug through enough historical traumas for several lifetimes. At parties, people talk about their vacations to the beach, and I want to tell them about the oddity of the pizza place across the street from Auschwitz or how the steward on the ill-fated ship *Edmund*

Fitzgerald was named Robert Rafferty. Until I met Elizabeth, I worried that I'd never feel close enough to anyone with whom to walk down the aisle. Now I've met her, and she's broken through my fears and defenses. The irony is that there's no aisle, just a beach at dawn.

I agree with Elizabeth; our honeymoon should be filled with fun and relaxation, not meditations on the horrors of war. And yet she recognizes that because I am me—me, who slows down for roadside history markers; me, who won a grant to travel anywhere in the world and went to Polish death camps; me, with two grandfathers who fought in the Pacific theater—I have a need to visit these two sites while we're in the islands.

* * *

Which explains why we're at the National Park Service–administered Pearl Harbor Visitor Center less than twenty-four hours before our wedding. I'm sitting on a bench outside the bathrooms, ticket in hand, waiting for the call to board the boat that will take us to the USS *Arizona* Memorial. Elizabeth, Jenn, and Jeremy are circulating somewhere.

I'm thinking of a story my grandmother Gigi told me. I'd asked her once while visiting her how she and my grandfather, who had died when I was five, had met.

"Well, he was a meat cutter at Milgram's, you know," Gigi said. "My mother would send me to do the shopping, because when I saw him, I'd ask him if he had a little extra meat for me."

She laughed. I gaped in shock at the idea of my grandmother flirting so brazenly. I've seen their wedding picture, with her in white and him in his navy blues, six feet plus, a beanpole of a man, as I was for a long time. She's lovely in that 1940s-war-bride way, her smile guileless and unafraid, although she must have known that there was a chance her groom would never come back from duty. Or that when he did come back, he'd wake screaming in the middle of the night, haunted by what he'd seen in the Pacific Ocean.

I look up from the ground and turn my head toward Pearl Harbor. Out on the water, sparkling in the sun, I can see the white docking quays, flat structures in the water marking the sites of boats sunk in the attack. A boat full of tourists buzzes by, returning to the visitor center dock. It's just beautiful outside, a brochure picture for the Aloha State.

I'm getting married tomorrow, I think. *My grandmother died yesterday.*

MONDAY, AUGUST 4

It's predawn, pitch black outside, only the streetlights along the Kalanianaole Highway punctuating the drive with a steady rhythm. To my left is the inky water of the ocean. I pass the sign for Hanauma Bay, where we snorkeled two days ago, and feel my heart drop a little bit. I turn up the radio and drive on, streetlight after streetlight, bursts of light in the darkness.

I'm alone in the final hours before my marriage. Elizabeth is currently in the makeup room at Captain Howie's, and now I'm heading back to Waikiki to pick up Jenn and Jeremy at their hotel.

This road is a pleasure to drive, curving around the southeastern tip of the island, and the convertible top ripples with a purr. I merge onto the interstate, then Kapiolani Boulevard. I say the name, sounding each syllable out loud: *ka-pi-o-la-ni.* Elizabeth—who can buy museum tickets in Berlin and get complimented on her German—mushes her way through the longer Hawaiian words, but I love the simplicity hidden in the language, the secret combination of just five vowels and eight consonants, thirteen letters that can say everything.

I have to believe that language is everything, that language can change things. In a few hours Elizabeth and I will change ourselves just by speaking. "I do," I'll say, and "I do," she'll say, and then Captain Howie will say, "I now pronounce you man and wife," and then suddenly we are not as we were before.

Pronounced husband and wife. Pronounced *ka-pi-o-la-ni*. Pronounced dead.

I say it again.

I turn onto Kalakaua Avenue, the sun rising in the rearview mirror.

SUNDAY, AUGUST 3

I'm always a little nervous on boats. Not because I think they'll sink and I'll drown—even Kansans can learn to swim—but because the pitch and the yaw of the boat, any boat, sends my stomach into knots and me to the rail.

But the ferry boat to the USS *Arizona* Memorial is navy-commanded and, as such, runs shipshape, steadily chugging along over toward Ford Island. The minimalist memorial spanning the wreckage of the *Arizona* gleams in the sun, curving gently in the center, representative of the weight of war. The word that comes to my mind is "soft," for some reason, although it's built from poured concrete, designed to resist the saltwater of the harbor.

Visible above the water are the ship's gun towers, rusted after almost sixty-seven years of exposure. Before boarding the ferry, we'd watched a short movie in the visitor center. Part of it was film, shot by a doctor on a nearby vessel, of the *Arizona* exploding. It's silent footage, black-and-white. A man's hand enters the frame, pointing at the sky, as the foredeck explodes, spreading black-and-white smudges across half of the ship.

Eleven hundred seventy-seven people died on the ship, which is still designated as an active military cemetery.

My own grandfather—Gigi's husband—served on the USS *Coos Bay,* a seaplane tender. It was a small ship as far as ships go. It received two battle stars, and after the war it was loaned to the Coast Guard, who eventually wore down the ship to the point where the only use for it was to sink it in training exercises. Decommissioned and struck from the Naval Register, the *Coos Bay* was towed far out from the Virginia coast, where two ships and thirty-five planes sank it.

Elizabeth and I have just moved to Virginia, to a small town about an hour south of DC. Somewhere off the coast of our new home, covered with coral and sea life, lies the boat on which my grandfather thought of my grandmother, the girl he'd marry someday.

We think of history as a colossus, a giant force sweeping the universe along, but the human scope of it is amazingly small. I'm writing this essay in 2012, four years after that three-day Hawaiian stretch in August. When I was fourteen, in 1990, my great-grandmother died; she was born in 1898. My mother was a fifteen-year-old when T. S. Eliot died. I shared the planet with Mao Zedong for five months. The last veteran of the First World War died just last year. Everything feels mushed together.

In Hawaii I am reading Abigail Thomas's memoir *A Three Dog Life,* about how she and her husband coped after a debilitating accident in which his brain was severely damaged. She writes, "The only way to contain catastrophe is to cordon it off with dates, but the numbers mean nothing." She's wrong—they're deeply important. We order our lives with memorials and their numbers both big and small, a thousand intersections of time and space—real time and real spaces—that let us understand our lives as part of history, as history itself. A memorial reserves space, holds it apart from the rest of the world, but it also lets us into that world in a tiny way—enough of a breach in time's hold to blow the whole thing apart.

We arrive at the memorial and disembark. Another group of tourists step onto the boat, and it chugs away, leaving our small group on an artificial island of white concrete, straddling the ship. No one says much.

SATURDAY, AUGUST 2

I am steeling myself as we walk the streets of Waikiki, looking for a place for lunch. The voicemail is still unlistened to a few hours after we've finished snorkeling, and although there has been a slight thaw in the last week or so with my family, I still default to avoidance whenever they're involved. My phone feels like a brick in my pocket.

Our friends are leading us toward a restaurant in a hotel that they've heard is good. Elizabeth is chatting with them. I drop behind.

OK, I think. *I should listen to this, get it over with.* Then I look up and have the frisson of recognizing a building I've never seen before. It's the Royal Hawaiian Hotel, Didion's hotel from "In the Islands," its pink façade gleaming in the sun. In the essay Didion writes that "only at the Royal Hawaiian" does she remember "a life so secure in its traditional concerns that the cataclysms of the larger society disturb it only as surface storms disturb the sea bottom, a long time later and in oblique ways." It is an enclave, sealed off from the world by distance and time and wealth.

I flip my phone open and press the voicemail button.

"Colin, it's your father."

I'm a little surprised to hear him.

"Some bad news. Your grandmother Braun died this morning."

He keeps talking, but I miss it, not with the shock of death, but because my first thought is *Who is he talking about? Grandmother Braun? He means Gigi, right?* My sister and I never called our mother's mother "Grandmother" or "Grandma" or anything like that. Instead, we called her Gigi, a mashed-up version of "Grandma" and "Margie" that our cousin invented as a toddler. I've literally never heard anyone refer to her as "Grandmother Braun" until this moment.

And then I realize: Gigi's dead. I'm staring at Didion's Royal Hawaiian Hotel, having just been "in the immutable pleasant rhythms of a life that used to be," and now Gigi's dead, and I realize that I will remember this place and this moment, this intersection of time and space, for the rest of my life.

SUNDAY, AUGUST 3

I'm looking out from the *Arizona* memorial at the wreckage of the ship, rusted except for the flagpole attached to the mast. What's left is close to the surface of the water, visible enough to make out a rough outline of the ship's features. A small iridescent pool appears on the surface of the water—a blob of oil from the hatches.

More than seven decades later, the *Arizona* still leaks a gallon or two of oil each day. When it was sunk, the ship held 1.5 million gallons, and in 2006 the National Park Service estimated that .5 million gallons remained, slowly spilling four drops each minute from several breaches in the ship's hull. Even at 2 gallons a day, enough oil remains to connect visitors to the fact of the ship's destruction, that single day in 1941, for hundreds of years to come.

Plenty of visitors have mythologized these leaks as the "black tears of the *Arizona*," but this metaphor seems sentimental. Instead, the oil strikes me as the inescapability of history, the fact that it cannot be contained, that it will seep out of any possible escape into the world. That no matter what we do to try to stop it, to set aside a site as a memorial, to cover wreckage with stone and steel, the fact of history will always remind us of the reality of the situation. At the *Arizona,* no one stops the oil from leaking, no one even suggests that we plug the leaks, which must be detrimental to the surrounding sea life. Even when the divers take down the ashes of *Arizona* survivors who choose to be interred with their crewmen, they do not stop the leaks. Let the boat weep forever, they say.

We join the line to get on the boat that will take us back to the visitor center, to the relative safety of the gift shop and information booth. As I step onto the boat, I am thinking about grief, both fresh and old, about how we go on despite the impossible weight of history reminding us at every turn that we can never escape it.

SATURDAY, AUGUST 2

Elizabeth and I are floating in the warm waters of Hanauma Bay, and I can't believe the life that's here. I've snorkeled before, but it's always been disappointing, facedown in murky water as a few tiny fish dart by. Today, though, in this place, I understand. Hundreds, thousands of brilliantly colored fish swim around us, over and through the giant coral reef of the bay. It's a Cousteau documentary here, and I'm content to float lazily while watching the scene.

Elizabeth reaches over and touches my arm. I look at her, and she points directly beneath us. A sea turtle, giant and oddly majestic, swims underneath, its flippers slowly propelling it forward through the ocean. I give Elizabeth a thumbs up. The gesture feels a little goofy, but it's the only way I can think of to show my gratitude for pointing this out to me. I look back at the turtle as it makes its way through the water.

In a hospital room in Missouri, a nurse monitors the suddenly dropping vital signs of my grandmother. Soon the doctor will pronounce the time of her death. Soon my phone will light up, its ringtone unheard in the glove box as we swim on, unaware, the clock ticking and the universe moving toward its inexorable moment when time and space, writing and memory, will intersect permanently on a sidewalk in front of the Royal Hawaiian Hotel.

SUNDAY, AUGUST 3

We're at Punchbowl Crater, the home of the National Memorial Cemetery of the Pacific. From the gate a field of green stretches in front of us, flanked on both sides by hundreds of white tombstones, and beyond those the sides of the crater, rising up all around us.

There are a few notable internments here, like war correspondent Ernie Pyle and *Challenger* astronaut Ellison Onizuka, but for the most part the men and women buried here are average

American soldiers, unified and made the same by death. For once, I don't want to seek out the famous graves or the most impressive memorials. Instead, I just want to walk around somewhere lovely that happens to be a necropolis.

When Didion visited the Punchbowl, they were digging graves at the very edge of the crater, and she witnessed the burial of a young man, "one of 101 Americans killed that week in Vietnam."

Most of the burials that take place here now are internments of cremains. Space has caught up after a long time; too many wars, too many dead. In a few days my grandmother will be cremated and buried next to my grandfather, reunited after twenty-seven years. There is plenty of space in the small cemetery in the small town where they lived. I will not be there for the ceremony, my family having told me that it will be small and short, no need to fly back. Just close family—there's an implication there.

"All I can tell you about the next ten minutes is that they seemed a very long time," Didion writes of the burial she observed.

We walk up a path along the side of the crater, looking for a view of Honolulu. From the top, next to the Memorial Walk, the view is beautiful, but I keep looking back at the Punchbowl and the map that we picked up at the entrance. From above, from the map, the National Memorial Cemetery of the Pacific looks like a CAT scan of a human brain slicing through the dendrites and axons of memory and understanding.

Death is Hamlet's "undiscovered country," and Hawaii is the farthest west I've ever been. When I worry about growing older, I worry about neurological disorders (although it is my heart that will likely kill me). I worry about forgetting, about not remembering, about the things I hold most dear slipping away from me.

Sand though fingers is a cliché, but I am on an island, surrounded by sand, standing on the edge of a volcano that will never explode again, and I am thinking about my brain burning out, my heart seizing up, my lungs collapsing. I want so desperately to think of beauty and love in that last moment, whenever it is, and what I want to think about, in that final moment of time, is Elizabeth.

MONDAY, AUGUST 4

And then finally, time and place have intersected at the moment that I want to remember. When I am old, memory failing, I want to remember these things, hold on to them until the very end: Elizabeth in her dress, the early morning sun falling upon it; taking off my shoes and socks and stepping onto the beach in a suit, the sand soft under my feet; the impossible blue of the water, nothing I'd ever seen before, in Kansas or elsewhere; the bursts of joyous laughter from all of us when Captain Howie asks me if I take Jenn instead of Elizabeth; and everyone speaking words, words that change the world, words that bring us into a new state of being, that join the two of us together for life, until death shall us part.

There doesn't have to be a memorial for this, no concrete structure holding the universe together in its memory, no stone or steel to bind this spot to that moment in time. I don't have to chase this moment down the way I have with dozens of other places and memories. This one is good, a moment in my life when I know who I am and what I am doing here.

A photo from that morning shows Elizabeth and me walking hand in hand down the beach. I think the photograph is beautiful, although I imagine it ranks high on the list of "Hawaii Wedding

Photos." After taking the picture, Captain Howie digitally erased every footstep on the beach, so after the fact, we are the only people who have made a mark on the world that single bright morning, August 4, 2008, a day shining and new, the universe opening up once again, not for the memory of the past, but for the endless possibilities of the future.

Phantoms (A Correspondence)

Dear Walsh,

The last two mornings, my wife and I have woken to a scurrying sound over our heads, and the last two afternoons, I've pulled down the attic ladder and climbed up to see what's there that shouldn't be there, roaming around the flattened cardboard boxes we stored when we moved to Fredericksburg almost two years ago.

Today I went up, hammer and stapler and scissors in my pocket and a roll of screening under my arm, and I duck-walked under the roof beams, past the boxes the previous tenant abandoned, to the windows on either end of our rental house, where something tore away the screens and bent the thin metal slats enough to fit through. I went up so that I could affix new barriers to our house, another bulwark against invaders.

Walsh, I'm trying to remember if we had Mr. Dillon's history class together, and if we learned about the Civil War in it. I find that now, fifteen years since we graduated, so much of high school has escaped my memory—things like the quadratic equation and the exact point of *Marbury v. Madison,* the Council of Trent, and almost anything I did in student council.

I remember you looking older than you actually were, a freshman who could have stepped onto an assembly line and picked up a welding gun right away. You drove a black car, a hand-me-down from some relative, I always guessed, with a Dead Kennedys bumper sticker, and I was intimidated by you and your fuck-you cool. I can't remember how we got to be friends. People in common, maybe.

Anyway, Walsh, the reason I bring up the Civil War is because I now live within a twenty-minute drive of four major battlefields. I teach in a building that's next to Confederate artillery earthworks, walk our dog down the Sunken Road that the Union soldiers tried and failed to take, and run along Stonewall Jackson's trench lines, still visible in the earth after 150 years. In Mr. Dillon's class the war felt abstract, a notion, "Bleeding Kansas" and John Brown and all those things that they used to try to connect it back to where we lived. I don't know about you, but it was always arrows on a map to me. Grant moves *here;* Lee moves *here;* Stuart rides *here.*

But, Walsh, I get it now. I've run up the hill of Marye's Heights, thinking about doing it under fire. I've stood at the point at Chancellorsville where Jackson's soldiers burst out onto Hooker's unsuspecting soldiers, scattering them, scarring them. I've visited

Gettysburg, just a little north of us, driven from the start of Pickett's Charge to the spot where it fell back, and I have to admit that at that spot, the whole thing—the romanticism of the Lost Cause of the South, the reenactors who loiter on my town's sidewalks when the battle anniversaries approach, the sentimentality of a sacrifice I never believed in—all made sense to me.

I keep waiting for you to call bullshit on me. Our first year, before we were friends, our school held a prayer service for soldiers in the Persian Gulf conflict. My cousin was in the navy, and I read his name into the microphone in our darkened gymnasium, a nervous freshman. I felt uncomfortable with the whole saber-rattling of those days, of President Bush (the first) announcing that the "world could wait no longer," of the *oohs* and *aahs* that accompanied the footage of the tracer bullets streaking across the Baghdad night sky.

Where were you then? Were you in the bleachers with everyone else, bored, scanning the rows of championship banners that hung from the rooftops? Had you already snuck out, smoking alone in the January cold of the Kansas winter we hated, that we would both find a way out of?

I find it hard to imagine, but do anyway: you might have thought then about joining the military. You might have imagined then—although it seems unlikely—that another Bush might send you to Iraq, that you would die in the flash of a roadside bomb.

I want to apologize, Walsh, for not knowing for three years that you had died. I didn't keep up with anyone after high school, so desperate to get away from Kansas that I ran all over the country, abandoning everyone in the process. Mostly I don't regret doing so—it saved me a fortune in wedding presents for people to whom I was only ever loosely attached—but still, for three years after you'd died, I thought you were alive. Getting ready to teach and picking a book off the shelf not far from the book of poetry you told me I should buy: I thought you were alive. Driving with my wife, hearing the radio play the song you told me about months before it broke big, suddenly everyone we disdained singing along: I thought you were alive. Standing in the bleachers at games, remembering you at our graduation breakfast, saying, "I'm so glad not everything's going to be about fucking sports anymore": I thought you were alive.

And you weren't. For three years, I went on like this, creating a version of you that didn't exist. And I want to say that if I didn't know that you were dead, then you were still alive. The sentimentality of a sacrifice I didn't believe in.

I keep trying to remember the last time I would have seen you; probably during that summer, before I left for college. I would have been dating Gina M. then; we would have seen you at one of the shows in someone's garage. But I can't be sure.

Walsh, I don't know who figures these things out, but I apparently live in the most haunted city in America. So many dead soldiers, dead civilians, walking around the streets of Fredericksburg. I don't believe in ghosts, but I wouldn't mind seeing you one more time.

Do you know the story of Stonewall Jackson's arm? He was wounded by his own men at Chancellorsville—a case of mistaken identity—and his arm had to be amputated. Someone walking past the hospital tent retrieved his arm, and they buried it in the family cemetery. I visited it two weeks ago on a beautiful November day, the cemetery surrounded by dried cornstalks. If it hadn't been for the hills, I would have sworn I was back in Kansas.

The war that you died in has been great for the prosthetics industry; medical science has advanced to the point where an injury that would have been fatal ten years ago is now just an amputation. *Good,* I think, *fewer widows, fewer orphans.* But how many memories of lost limbs, how many unscratchable itches on thighs and elbows missing? So much phantom pain from what's no longer there.

Walsh, it's late, and I should get to bed. My wife is already there, sleep mask on, dog at her feet. Whatever ghost is in our attic sleeps too, having made it past the screen I tacked up this afternoon. And you—you're somewhere out there, too, at rest in what you are, and no longer are, a phantom, a shadow cast along the fields in the daytime.

Your friend,
Colin

Reflecting Mirror

ORLANDO, THE DAY AFTER

I want the light to shine through.

* * *

My wife and I are in Orlando—the Kennedy Space Center, actually, an hour out from the Land of the Mouse—and in front of me stands the massive Astronaut Memorial, tilted, tiled panels of black granite with names on them. It is the day after a tornado has hit Tuscaloosa, Alabama, passing through our old neighborhood, destroying the houses around the house in which we used to live, killing dozens. I am trying not to think about this too much, trying not to think about how had we not moved to Virginia three years ago, I might have opened my front door this morning to a landscape of destruction, of trees bent and broken, roofs peeled off and scattered a state away.

* * *

So I am thinking about dead astronauts instead, here at the Astronaut Memorial. This is what I do in time of trauma, when I cannot put together the facts of the problem in front of me: I put together the facts of some other problem. The space program is so good at this, at figuring out what went wrong. *Apollo I:* an oxygen-rich environment bursts into flames. *Challenger:* low temperatures warp the O-rings, allowing hot gases to compromise the external fuel tank. *Columbia:* debris at launch damaged the shuttle's wing, leading to the vehicle's breakup upon reentry.

* * *

This could happen with the tornado, too. Meteorology could explain why the wind and humidity started spinning around each other faster and faster, why it turned at the stadium to head into the Forest Lake neighborhood, maybe even why it just blew a branch into the living room window of my old house instead of tearing it down so that no stone stood atop another, the way it did with houses a block away.

But too much will remain unknown, more than mathematics and simulation models could ever reveal. There will be no explanation for why the tornado took a path through the working-class neighborhoods, why it stayed on the ground for so long, dragging its massive self across the town, erasing so much of what I knew about my wife's hometown, my adopted town.

* * *

Known: the final words spoken on the shuttle.
Unknown: the final words spoken in the house.

* * *

I can't put any of this together in my head, so I am looking at the Astronaut Memorial. It is a tilted set of black granite tiles, a reflecting mirror. The tiles have the names of deceased astronauts carved into them—some I know, some I don't. Some I learn about only because of this memorial, those who died in test flights and car wrecks and commercial plane crashes.

Each name is golden, bright, and I learn later that when the memorial was first built, it turned so that the sun would reflect off parabolic mirrors through the names, illuminating them. However, after a few years, the motors broke down, and now the names are illuminated artificially, lights shining on them even on a day as bright as the one on which my wife and I are visiting.

I want to think about this light most of all, the way that light moves through a landscape to commemorate the dead, to say that they are remembered. I want to think about the names I know, the names I have just learned, the names I know are alive, and the names I will learn have died. I want to think about the house where my girlfriend and I returned to, engaged to be married; to think about the bedroom and how the light came in each morning. I want to think about a landscape torn apart, a district of destruction, a neighborhood about which my neighbor Andy, whose house survived solely because all the trees fell away from it, writes: *Without the trees, sunlight comes into the house in strange and unexpected ways.* I want to think about a parabolic mirror and broken motors and frozen O-rings and forecast models and how all of it, all of it, lets the light shine through.

Hallow This Ground

I'm from the Midwest; I know cold. As a child in Kansas, I once slid home from school on sheets of ice covering the sidewalks. When I lived in Iowa, I figured out a path from the edge of campus to my classroom that took me through as many buildings as possible, an escape from a wind chill so brutal that it could freeze nostrils shut.

And yet right now, in a parking lot in Maryland, I'm colder than I've been in years, a cold settling deep in my bones that I can't shake off. The car's dashboard shows just seven lines in its digital temperature readout, like lined-up toothpicks reading "7 F."

We could quadruple that number and still be below freezing. And while it gets cold—below freezing, even—in Alabama, the state that Elizabeth and I moved from just eight months ago, it never gets this cold there.

Perhaps what I said earlier is wrong. I *knew* cold. I've forgotten it.

I look over to the passenger seat, where Elizabeth sleeps or, maybe like me, tries to sleep. We got up before dawn to drive from our house in Fredericksburg, Virginia, to a country club in Maryland, where her father, director of tennis for a city in Alabama, is giving a clinic for other tennis pros, and we're trying to catch a few winks before we pick him up at the end of his presentations.

If he weren't also one of the kindest and most generous people I know, I'd be tempted to characterize my father-in-law as a workaholic. He works just about every single day and has managed to visit us from Alabama—our first family visitor in our new state—by scheduling this clinic in Maryland. We've promised to show him around Washington, DC, a town he's seen only in movies.

My father-in-law isn't the only visitor to the capital this weekend. In just four days, Barack Obama will be inaugurated as the forty-fourth president of the United States, and the city practically crackles with anticipation. In October, Obama and Joe Biden made a campaign stop at the school where I teach, a liberal arts college with an enrollment of just four thousand. Twenty-five thousand people turned out to see them speak in what a colleague called the biggest thing to happen in Fredericksburg since the Civil War.

And Obama had won Virginia, the first Democrat to do so since LBJ, thanks in part to a dedicated army of volunteers, me among them. I had knocked on doors and made phone calls, and on Election Day I had served as a poll watcher for the Democrats, making sure that voters could cast their ballots without hassles. In the final minutes of the election, I helped get one last voter into the booth. Whatever I could do for the campaign—for America, really.

I had wanted to love the United States again, the way I did when I was a Boy Scout. The Bush years had worn that love down to a grudging belief that things might be OK again someday, that eventually we would be able to travel abroad without apologizing for our country, that we might not send soldiers—our friends and family—into preemptive wars. In Alabama, Elizabeth and I had weathered the very edge of Hurricane Katrina and seen the waves of evacuees enter the town while the commentators on television looked at the footage from New Orleans and Mississippi and marveled, "Is this America?"

"This is America now, yes," I said back to the screen.

It feels very naïve to write all this now, in Obama's second term. Hindsight lets me know that we were always going to be disappointed, that the problems with America could not be erased, only halted in some cases and ignored in others. But that morning in Maryland, cold as we were, there was a warm feeling, not yet mocked by Republicans, a feeling that we understood to be an unfamiliar notion called "hope."

Elizabeth stirs, asks the time. I tell her.

"We should probably head over there," she says.

I start the car, grateful for the blast of air coming from the heater. I shift out of park and drive out of the lot.

It is morning in America.

* * *

"They're saying that they expect two million people for the inauguration," Elizabeth says from the backseat as we head into the District.

"Unbelievable," her father says.

I guide the car over the bridge, toward the National Mall. The temperature has finally reached double digits.

"I'll see if we can find a spot to park next to the Department of Agriculture, but we'll probably have to find somewhere farther away and walk in." Two million people showing up in three days means we'll most likely have to pay to park.

And yet—a miracle of hope!—when I turn onto Jefferson Drive, an empty spot is right there in front of the Department of Agriculture, the best possible parking space in DC for walking around the National Mall's monuments and memorials.

A few minutes later we're bundling up in the coats, hats, and scarves we brought from home for today. Although it's still below freezing, it feels significantly warmer. Elizabeth looks over at her father, who's wearing only his thin army jacket.

"Dad, are you sure you don't want something else? We've got extra gloves and scarves if you want."

"I'm OK," he says. "I've got the army jacket."

I admire his imperviousness to cold. We shut the trunk.

"Everyone ready?" I ask. "This way, then."

We head to the crosswalk, toward the obelisk of the Washington Monument.

* * *

One of the side effects of learning a bunch of things is that my head is crammed with them all the time. I used to think of my memory as a giant card catalog, thousands of index cards cross-indexed against each other. Now I think of it as a waterslide that twists and turns, leading down through a dozen angles to where it could have reached much more quickly had it just gone from *A* to *B*.

This tendency is usually annoying, but it's tremendously useful when I get to play tour guide, like I am right now, pointing out the spot on the Washington Monument, about one-third of the way up, where the color of the stone changes slightly.

"Construction got held up in the first part of the nineteenth century for a few reasons," I say. "Lots of groups had donated stones for the construction, and anti-Catholic groups actually stole the stone that the Vatican sent."

My father-in-law looks up the obelisk. A circle of flapping flags surrounds us, snapping in the wind. From our vantage point at the top of this small hill, I point out our path, saying that we'll head down past the World War II Memorial, along one side of the Reflecting Pool to the Lincoln Memorial, then around the Tidal Basin through the FDR Memorial to the Jefferson Memorial.

After I point out our path, I look across to the White House. Even though I've visited DC a few times since we moved to Virginia, I've avoided the White House as a protest—quiet, useless—against its current occupant. But now, with four days left in his presidency, I feel only a mild apathy toward Bush. He's irrelevant now. What can he do besides issue a few pardons?

My father-in-law looks out at the White House with me. Not looking at me, he speaks. "Well, Colin, do you think Obama can do it?"

We've never spoken about politics before this moment. To our left, across the drained Reflecting Pool, a large stage stands ready for tomorrow's star-studded concert. In a landscape obsessed with the past, it is strange to think about the future.

"I wouldn't have voted for him if I didn't think so," I say. "I hope he can."

My father-in-law makes a noncommittal sound. I don't know how he voted, although John McCain won Alabama with 60 percent of the vote. And yet my father-in-law is so giving of himself, the least greedy person I know, that I don't care how he voted. He is a man who, as Lincoln put it, is guided by the "better angels of his nature."

* * *

As we walk along the empty Reflecting Pool, shivering in the wind, I look up toward the stage in front of the Lincoln Memorial. Some figures, too small to distinguish, move around on the stage, and a few echoes from the microphones spread out over the gray sky. I realize, a little disappointed, that the stage blocks the steps leading up to Lincoln.

"Looks like we can't get into Lincoln," I say to Elizabeth and her father. "The stage for that concert tomorrow is blocking it, and it sounds like they're doing a sound check right now."

We reach the entrance to the Vietnam Veterans Memorial and begin to descend the ramp alongside the wall. Soon the names of the dead and missing are over our heads.

"I had simple impulse to cut into the earth," wrote Maya Lin in the fall of 1982. "I imagined taking a knife and cutting into the earth, opening it up, an initial violence that in time would heal. The grass would grow back, but the initial cut would remain a pure flat surface in the earth with a polished, mirrored surface, much like the surface on a geode when you cut it and polish the edge. The need for the names to be on the memorial would become the memorial; there was no need to embellish the design further. The people and their names would allow everyone to respond and remember."

Lin's design, radical enough at the time to make some veterans' groups demand a more realistic, representative memorial statue, has become the standard now. Once we memorialized the group; now we memorialize the individuals. The field of 168 chairs in Oklahoma City, the benches of the Pentagon Memorial, the names engraved in the winning design for the World Trade Center Memorial.

When they build the memorial for the Iraq and Afghanistan wars, they'll put the names on those, too. We'll gather there and find our loved ones, the absence a physical cut into stone or steel.

At the wall, my father-in-law seems distracted, talking as we move through the memorial. When he visits again a few months later, he'll look up a name in the guidebooks at the entrance, searching for a name my wife has never heard but shares.

"Do you want to find him?" I'll ask.

"Aw, it's OK," he'll say. "We can keep going."

I will want to see this name, want to have a proxy connection to one of the names on the wall, but I'll quickly recognize that perhaps my wife's father would like to remember his classmate as alive, and not as a name engraved in letters, .53 inches high on a wall.

That's in the future. Now the wall acts as a wind tunnel, and the cold feels even worse down here.

We move on up from the depths toward the Lincoln Memorial.

* * *

I'm disappointed that we can't reach the Lincoln Memorial. It's always the monument on the mall that never loses power for me. Every time I go there, I'm in awe at the quiet majesty of the seated sixteenth president, the hands modeled on life casts of Lincoln's own, the size of the columns, the marker for the spot where Martin Luther King Jr. delivered his "I Have a Dream" speech, and the engraved texts on the interior walls of the memorial, the Gettysburg Address on one side, the second inaugural address on the other.

I read both every time I'm inside those walls, taking the time to scan the speeches carefully. The second inaugural address, delivered just one month and ten days before his assassination, is a beautiful model for how we should be as a country, the interconnected nature of each individual who makes up America. Here is a man exhausted by war—just compare the photos of him in 1860 from those in 1865—but who looks forward to the reconciliation that is much closer than it was a year and a half earlier, when he stood in a cemetery in a small Pennsylvania town and delivered a speech of only 270 words.

The reason for Lincoln's speech is to set aside the ground at Gettysburg to the memory of the men who fought and died there. However, the genius of it lies in his recognition that his words are redundant in the face of the greater sacrifice. "In a larger sense we can not dedicate—we can not consecrate—we can not hallow—this ground," he says to the assembled crowd in 1863. "The brave men living and dead who struggled here have consecrated it far above our poor power to add or detract," it reads on the south wall of the memorial in 2009.

"It is rather for us to be here dedicated to the great task remaining before us," Lincoln says. And here, on a cold January day, with an African American man about to take office in a building built by enslaved men, the task feels a little more complete. There is still the work to be done, but one man from Illinois is continuing the work that another man from Illinois did 148 years earlier.

* * *

We're missing all of this, of course. Walking along the sidewalk in front of the Lincoln Memorial, I see an old man on the stage in a gray stocking cap, holding a banjo. He strums a few notes while another man with an acoustic guitar walks toward him. The old man steps to the microphone and begins singing.

"As I went walking," he warbles, *"that ribbon of highway."* The banjo's chords are clean in the cold air. I realize that the old man is folk legend Pete Seeger practicing for tomorrow's concert with Woody Guthrie's "This Land Is Your Land," a song I've always thought captured the American ideal better than our actual national anthem.

I'm about to point this out to Elizabeth and her father when the next verse begins, sung by the other man in a lower, more gravelly voice. Elizabeth stops in her tracks.

She is not given to stopping in her tracks.

"I know that voice!" she says, noticeably excited. "That's Springsteen!"

The three of us turn toward the stage. There, on stage, with seated Mr. Lincoln visible behind him, is Bruce Springsteen, my wife's favorite musician, singing "This Land Is Your Land" with Pete Seeger.

It's an impossible moment. No way could we have planned this for my father-in-law's first visit to Washington. Two of America's best singer-songwriters, men who have defined American music in two different generations, are on stage, working together to sing one of America's best songs.

“Unbelievable,” my father-in-law says again. I agree. The cold has vanished. I think of the moment during Lincoln’s second inaugural, recorded by several attendees, in which the sun, absent for so long in the Washington sky, broke through the clouds. Above us an endless skyway, below us a golden highway, in a land made for you and me.

* * *

The sound check finishes. We pass through the larger-than-life soldiers of the Korean War Veterans Memorial and across Independence Avenue, entering the Franklin Delano Roosevelt Memorial, the largest in area of the memorials in the National Mall/Tidal Basin area. It’s Elizabeth’s favorite memorial by far, and I let her take the lead in guiding her father through it.

The memorial is divided into four open-air “rooms,” four spaces symbolizing each of FDR’s four terms. Several bronze statues fill each room, as do spaces for water, which, unfortunately, are turned off to avoid making the space treacherous with ice.

“You’ll have to come back and see it when the water’s on, Dad,” Elizabeth says. “It’s just stunning.”

I follow a little bit behind them, reading the quotations carved into the stone of the memorial.

“No country, however rich, can afford the waste of its human resources. Demoralization caused by vast unemployment is our greatest extravagance. Morally, it is the greatest menace to our social order,” reads a stone in the first room, and I remember that when FDR took office in March 1933, one-quarter of Americans were unemployed. Right now, in January 2009, that rate is 7.8 percent, and we still feel like we’re headed over the precipice.

I realize I'm on a pilgrimage here. I'm walking through reminders of the times when the American president saved the country. Roosevelt, like Lincoln, like Washington, was the right president at the right time. America would have been a much different country had Washington not turned down the chance of unlimited power, had Lincoln not shifted the focus of the war from the rebellion to slavery and rededicated the country to its original "proposition that all men are created equal," had Roosevelt not decided that the country had a moral obligation to provide jobs and care for its citizens.

And I also realize I'm hoping that Obama is that kind of president, the right man at the right time. In a room of a memorial dedicated to the last time the Democrats saved the country, I find myself thinking what could be an American prayer: *Let this country be what it promises to be; let it fulfill Roosevelt's oath of "We have faith that future generations will know that here, in the middle of the twentieth century, there came a time when men of goodwill found a way to unite, and produce, and fight to destroy the forces of ignorance, and intolerance and slavery and war." Let this be that time, too.*

I've fallen behind Elizabeth and her father, who are already to the last room. We have just a single memorial to go, and with the sun setting on the day, the temperature is dropping once again.

* * *

We make our way around the Tidal Basin, taking care not to bump our heads on the cherry tree branches that grow over the sidewalk. I can see our final destination, the Jefferson Memorial, ahead in the fading light. By the time we reach the steps leading up to the Palladian dome, the sun is gone, and the glow from the inside draws us close.

I never took the apparently standard high school trip to Washington, DC. The only time I'd been here as a child was with my family when I was five. I have only a handful of memories from that visit that I can be sure are mine: a movie at the Air and Space Museum, waiting in the car at Arlington National Cemetery, and standing in the Jefferson Memorial, reading the words of the Declaration of Independence on the wall.

Here I am again, twenty-seven years later, reading those same words. After all the history and hope that we've walked through today, it's enough to send a frisson down my spine, noticeably different from the chills I've grown used to today.

"We hold these truths to be self-evident: that all men are created equal, that they are endowed by their Creator with certain inalienable rights, among these are life, liberty, and the pursuit of happiness," I read again. It's the second time today I've encountered Jefferson's words. Previously, in the Gettysburg Address at the Lincoln Memorial, they were a challenge to live up to; here, though, back at the time when America is just a radical idea—let the governed, even if it's just the white landowning males, rule themselves—those words feel more like a promise.

I'm a child of America's bicentennial, born in 1976, another time when eight years of Republican rule and a quagmire war had left the country weary. There'll never be a monument erected to the president elected that year, who was not the chief executive the country needed at that time. But I still grew up in a family of Midwestern New Deal Democrats, people who believed that one of the government's main jobs was to protect citizens from the excesses of business and, failing that, to help them until they were able to help themselves.

In an early draft of the Declaration, Jefferson wrote "life, liberty, and the pursuit of property," but scratched out the last word in favor of "happiness." We are always writing America into existence: Lincoln, Roosevelt, Jefferson, Maya Lin, even me with this simple essay about a cold day walking around the capital city. America is a country made by words, transformed by words, written over and over into each one of its citizens. A country where every four years we gather in front of the Capitol, or the television, or the radio, to listen to words, to listen to a man (and one day, soon, I imagine, a woman) speak those words, speaking a new version of the country into existence.

Right now, somewhere in this town, the president-elect and his team are writing a new America. I want to believe it is an America where *laws and institutions must go hand in hand with the progress of the human mind,* an America where the wounds are healing, an America where another generation *has a rendezvous with destiny,* an America where *we strive on to finish the work we are in.* I want to believe it is the America I feel tonight, more deeply than the cold all around us.

I want, I realize, to hope once more for this country, to hallow this ground. *This land is your land; this land is my land; this land was made for you and me.*

* * *

We circle back to the car and start it, turning the heater up as far as it will go, leaving our lucky space for the next tourists. We drive a loop around the mall, past each Smithsonian museum, and in front of the Capitol, where another stage has been built for Obama's inauguration. We can see the giant screens they've set up for the expected millions, and another familiar face is on them, singing another sound check into the night.

"That's Bono," Elizabeth says over the roar from the vents. "U2's playing here, too?"

"Unbelievable," my father-in-law says. "There's always something happening here."

I agree with him. It is unbelievable. I am ready to believe.

We cross over the Potomac River, back into Virginia, leaving behind a landscape of the past that reminds us of the future.

Aftermath

A CONCLUSION

Another day, another empty field.

Except not really—by this point in my life it's never an empty field. A wooden fence, rough-hewn, zigzags its way across my edge of the field in front of a forest. A path, muddy from the earlier rain, rolls up and down the field's dips. My dog sniffs around the base of a sapling and raises his leg to urinate on it.

The fence is interrupted every hundred feet or so by large stone markers. They look like tombstones but are bigger, taller than I am. Each one reads "IOWA."

I'm in Tennessee.

Across the field—a few hundred feet, I'd say, but I've never been good at estimating distance—I can see a row of cannon, dozens of them, each pointed toward me and the Iowa markers.

It's the second week of 2012. Almost 150 years ago—149 years, 10 months, and 1 day, to be exact—Confederate troops charged across this field eleven times, trying to take the Iowans' position. Eleven times across this empty field, eleven times advancing over the bodies of their comrades, eleven times withdrawing back to their original line.

The Iowans held their position until their flanks collapsed under the attacks of other Confederates, as well as an artillery barrage from sixty-two cannon across the field, the largest array ever on an American battlefield. General Benjamin Prentiss gave the command to withdraw, but as the Iowa soldiers tried to escape through the woods, the Confederates closed in from both sides, surrounding them. More than twenty-two hundred Union soldiers were taken prisoner, including Prentiss.

The dog and I move down the fence. He sniffs around while I read the text on every marker. Each one commemorates a regiment of infantry, numbering the original strength of the regiment as well as its wounded and killed. The closer we get to the center of the fence, the higher the number of captured recorded. Of the 442 men of the 14th Iowa Volunteer Infantry Regiment ("including musicians, teamsters, etc."), only 8 men were killed and 39 wounded. Two hundred twenty-six were taken prisoner.

I look down at the dog. He looks up at me and wags his tail.

I'm happy, too.

* * *

It's been over a decade since I stood outside Columbine High School. When I started paying serious attention to what had been a casual interest in monuments and memorials, I did it mostly as a way to move outside of myself, out of what I saw as an uninteresting existence. Taking on the physical manifestations of public memory would be a way, I reasoned, that I could look at history from a new perspective.

I did this because I didn't think I had anything within myself that was worthwhile. No trauma of my own, so I decided to adopt that of others. So I headed out across the country, even across the ocean, to visit "the places where."

I was young then; younger, at least. Now I'm old enough to run for president. I've graduated from an MFA program and gotten a tenure-track job. I moved from the Deep South to the Mid-Atlantic. I've taught hundreds of students, taking some of them out to the grave of Stonewall Jackson's arm so that I could give them a writing assignment that I would have loved.

The women I thought I would be with, either out of desire or just momentum, they all fell away, until there was one, the one I loved in a way I couldn't imagine existed until it did. I married Elizabeth in the rising sun on a beach in Hawaii. Two years later I stood next to her in a hospital room as her brother died. Four months after that we drove into her hometown to help it dig out after a tornado blasted through it, decimating our former neighborhood to the point where I couldn't recognize the streets on which we'd walked our dog.

I've been a pallbearer twice.

All this is to say I think enough things have happened to me that I don't think my original motivations for seeking out these monuments and memorials applies any longer.

* * *

So why am I here? The books and documentaries on the Civil War love to point out the irony of the name of this battlefield, that a "place of peace" could be the site of a two-day battle in which more American soldiers died than in all previous American wars combined. The real irony, I've learned, is that setting aside the sites of trauma does make them peaceful places. The most beautiful days of my weeks in Poland were at extermination camps. At Birkenau, not far from the site of the gas chambers, I watched a heron glide over the ruins of barracks chimneys, circling around and around on thermal updrafts. The monuments and memorials are on sites where, for a short time, chaos and destruction reign, followed by our recognition that those sites must be preserved. In preserving them we keep them pristine, untouched—and we make them beautiful in that way.

For a few days in 1862 Shiloh was a terrible place. And then we saved it and made it what its name said it was all along. And so I'm here, me and the dog, while Elizabeth is away at a conference, to see this place.

* * *

The dog and I drive along the roads of Shiloh, following in a rough chronology the push and pull of the two days. On the first day, Confederates pressed the surprised Union forces almost all the way back to the Tennessee River before Grant's army was able to stall them. Overnight, Don Carlos Buell's Army of the Ohio arrived at to reinforce Grant's men, and the next day the combined Union forces pushed the exhausted Confederates back to Shiloh Church and did not pursue the rebels as they withdrew to the rail junction at Corinth, Mississippi.

We pull up to another stop on the tour: #13, the Peach Orchard. The National Park Service brochure informs me that "Sarah Bell's orchard was in full bloom when Confederate troops attacked

Union forces here on April 6," the first day of fighting. It's overcast here now, and the peach trees—saplings, protected by triangles of wooden fencing—are bare.

They're regrowing the Peach Orchard at Shiloh. A careful reconstruction, but another small moment of beauty in a place once terrible.

As the dog and I are looking at the new peach trees, a car pulls in next to mine, the first tourists I've seen all day. The dog immediately wags his tail, and I decide to ask the new arrivals if they'll take our picture.

They agree, and I hand them my camera. In the picture I have a big smile on my face, and the dog sits at my feet, briefly pausing in his explorations. It's a good photo, a nice moment to fix and remember.

I thank the tourists and return to the car. I won't see anyone else in the park today, no one else to interrupt the peace.

* * *

The next stop on the tour is the Bloody Pond, which I remember from my grade school's unit on the Civil War. Wounded men and horses came here to drink, and often to die, and the water was stained red with their blood. Ambrose Bierce, who fought for the Union Army in the battle, described the scene:

> Knapsacks, canteens, haversacks distended with soaken and swollen biscuits, gaping to disgorge, blankets beaten into the soil by the rain, rifles with bent barrels or splintered stocks, waist-belts, hats and the omnipresent sardine-box—all the wretched debris of the battle still littered the spongy earth as far as one could see, in every direction. Dead horses were

> every-where; a few disabled caissons, or limbers, reclining on one elbow, as it were; ammunition wagons standing disconsolate behind four or six sprawling mules. Men? There were men enough; all dead.

I leave the dog in the car, and he watches me through the window as I walk over to the edge of the Bloody Pond. It's starting to rain, just a little bit, enough to make hundreds of small ripples appear in the water, concentric circles running into each other in dozens of different places.

At water's edge I squat down and look into the water. I can't say exactly why, but this feels momentous, more so than any other place I've been on this battlefield. I put my hand into the Bloody Pond. The water's cold. I press it into the mud and then wave it underwater, cleaning it. I realize that I am washing myself clean of the mud, that I am washing myself clean of all the history and traumas and memorials, of all the stone and steel and engraved names and abstract representations of real sorrows and atrocities, of all that I have tried to take on from that day in Colorado years ago when I stood in front of a high school, looking at its boarded-up library windows. I am not that person anymore.

* * *

I go back to the car. The dog, who hasn't moved from his post watching out the window, wags his tail as I approach. Looking at the map, I see we have just a handful of stops left before we return to the start of the loop road. Soon we'll leave this park and drive back into the world, back to the cities of the living. We'll arrive at the airport and stand outside the automatic doors and wait to be reunited with the woman we love.

NOTES

SURFACING

For more on the *Edmund Fitzgerald* and other shipwrecks on the Great Lakes, see Mark L. Thompson, *Graveyard of the Lakes* (Detroit: Wayne State University Press, 2004).

THE PATH

Quotes on the faulty design of the Kansas City Hyatt Regency are from Henry L. Petroski, *To Engineer Is Human: The Role of Failure in Successful Design* (New York: Random House, 1992).

VICTIMS: THE YELLOW FLOWERS

The concept of separating participants in the Holocaust into the three categories of "victims," "bystanders," and "perpetrators" is that of Raul Hilberg, author of *The Destruction of the European Jews* (New York: Holmes & Meier, 1985).

The fragmented sections are taken from interviews with individuals—victims, bystanders, and perpetrators—associated with the Treblinka extermination camp, as interviewed in Claude Lanzmann's 1985 documentary, *Shoah* (a co-production by Les Films Aleph and Historia Films with the assistance of the French Ministry of Culture, 1985).

The phrase "perhaps the most magnificent of Holocaust memorials" comes from James E. Young, *The Texture of Memory: Holocaust Memorials and Meaning* (New Haven, CT: Yale University Press, 1993).

BYSTANDERS: THE END OF THE WORLD

For Raul Hilberg's views on "Auschwitz's symbolic nature," see *Perpetrators, Victims, Bystanders: The Jewish Catastrophe, 1933–1945 (New York: Aaron Asher Books, 1992).*

The Robert Jan van Pelt quote is from Errol Morris's documentary *Mr. Death: The Rise and Fall of Fred A. Leuchter Jr.* (a co-production by Channel Four Films, Fourth Floor Pictures, Independent Film Channel, and Scout Productions, 2000).

For Victor Frankl, see *Man's Search for Meaning* (1946; New York: Pocket Books, 1963).

THIS DAY IN HISTORY

All the proposed memorials for the site of the World Trade Center are archived at the official website of the competition (http://wtcsitememorial.org/submissions.html), including the two proposals by Michael Arad and Peter Walker, which, after going through a revision process, became the memorial dedicated in 2011.

DOORS

In 2010 the University of Alabama dedicated Malone-Hood Plaza in front of Foster Auditorium, a commemorative space dedicated to the first two African American students at the school. Malone-Hood Plaza also features the Autherine Lucy Clock Tower, dedicated to the woman who attempted to integrate the school in 1956, but who was suspended and later expelled by the university, which said it could not protect her.

Foster Auditorium itself has been renovated and is now the site of sporting events and classes.

WHAT I WAS DOING THERE

Didion quotes are from Joan Didion, "In the Islands," in *The White Album* (New York: Macmillan, 1990). Thomas quote on dates is from Abigail Thomas, *A Three Dog Life* (San Diego: Harcourt, 2006).

HALLOW THIS GROUND

For designer Maya Lin's comments on the Vietnam Veterans Memorial, see Maya Lin, *Boundaries* (New York: Simon and Schuster, 2006).

AFTERMATH: A CONCLUSION

Ambrose Bierce's description of the battle at Bloody Pond is from Ambrose Bierce, "What I Saw of Shiloh," in *The Devil's Dictionary, Tales, and Memoirs* (New York: Library of America, 2011).

COLIN RAFFERTY was born in Kansas City, Missouri, and grew up on the Kansas side. He attended Kansas State University and Iowa State University, and he holds a Master of Fine Arts degree from the University of Alabama. He teaches creative writing at the University of Mary Washington and lives in Richmond, Virginia. This is his first book.

CPSIA information can be obtained at www.ICGtesting.com
Printed in the USA
LVOW10s0006140116
470476LV00009B/878/P

9 780253 019073